CRYPTO UNFILTERED

STORIES OF HYPE, LESSONS, AND THE DIGITAL FUTURE

VIPUL YADAV

notionpress.com

INDIA · SINGAPORE · MALAYSIA

ISBN
Paperback 979-8-90319-748-4
Hardcase 979-8-90362-393-8

Contents

Introduction

Welcome, reader.

Welcome to a world that's as puzzling as it is fascinating. A world that excites you one moment but unsettles you the next.

Welcome to the world of Cryptocurrency.

Often, change has a sneaky way of creeping into our lives. One day you're swiping your credit card like it's cutting-edge tech, and the next—boom!—people are buying virtual coins and calling it the future of money.

We live in one of those moments right now. The world around us is changing faster than ever before, so fast that we rarely notice the transformation until we find ourselves immersed in it. It's happening quietly, relentlessly, in the heart of our financial systems.

Bitcoin. Ethereum. NFTs. Buzzwords everywhere. Headlines screaming from news sites. Influencers hyping it up on YouTube. Even your cousin who still owes you $50 is suddenly a "crypto expert."

Over decades, the financial world has seen waves of innovation—credit cards, online banking, mobile payments. Each brought convenience. Each shaped the way we interact with money.

But this? This is different.

One day, you see tweets about overnight crypto millionaires, making you wonder why you're not on the crypto rocket yet. The next day, you hear horror stories of people losing their life savings, and thank the universe you stayed away.

Crypto isn't just for tech nerds anymore. It's shaping how we think about money, trust, and value. Yet, for most people, it's still a mystery.

Some call it the future. Others call it a scam. The rest simply ignore its existence.

The truth is – **Crypto is complicated.**

That's why this book exists—to make sense of it all. No jargon. No hype. Just real talk and hard-earned lessons from someone who's been there.

By the end, you'll know what this space really is and how to navigate it without losing your mind—or your money.

And here's the best part of it all. You don't need a finance degree to tag along. Just curiosity and an open mind. I'll handle the rest.

Think of this as a conversation, not a classroom. By the time you finish, you'll feel confident enough to explore, experiment, and maybe even invest—without feeling lost or overwhelmed.

Together, let's add another chapter to the ever-growing book of financial literacy.

Before we start, one quick disclaimer:

I've never promoted or endorsed any crypto project for personal gain. This book is not a sales pitch. It's a story—**my story.** And maybe, by the end, it'll become part of yours too.

As we explore this world together, you'll notice me using terms like cryptocurrencies, digital assets, coins, and tokens interchangeably. Don't get confused, as they all mean the same.

Oh, and one more thing—there are two pictures in this book. Their significance will become clear in time. For now, just know they're part of the story.

So, buckle up. Let's begin the ride!

As you scroll to the next chapter, I will be waiting in Texas, where my story and our journey are ready to take off.

1

My Dinner Date with Bitcoin

2015, *College Station, Texas, United States.*

By year seven of my IT job in India, my days felt like photocopies—same desk, same colleagues, same tasks. Boredom reached its limit, and my life desperately needed some spark.

I spoke to a few friends who offered the usual advice of "Hey, why don't you switch to a new company or try a different role?"

While the suggested options were worth considering, I was looking for something different. An experience more than just flipping Companies and Bosses.

This was when the idea of pursuing Higher Education in the U.S. sounded like the best path, given the options I had. With sincerity and dedication, I thus studied, gave my exams, and applied to a few reputed colleges until the day arrived when I finalized "Mays Business School, Texas A&M" as my next destination.

August 2015 arrived, and I was all but set to pack my bags and move to the "Land of Opportunities" to pursue my Master's in Information Systems.

The college was quite popular, and I, along with my family, was pretty satisfied with the decision.

Before I could catch my breath, 2015 had dissolved into memory and half of 2016 slipped quietly through my fingers, swept away by college duties, a part-time job, and endless house chores. Autumn whispered its farewell, and winter arrived like a silent guest at dusk.

And with that, arrived that memorable evening. The evening that kicked off my crypto journey. When a new chapter began in my life.

So, it begins.

The sun had slipped below the horizon earlier than usual, and the cold evening air reminded me to wrap up my part-time shift on our college campus. I grabbed my bag, hopped on my bicycle, and pedaled back toward my apartment.

Normally, my place was full of noise—roommates chatting, music playing—but lately it was quiet. They'd all left for winter break, and I stayed behind. The silence felt heavy, pressing against the walls, and for the first time in weeks, loneliness crept in.

Hungry and craving company, I decided to spend my evening at a close friend's place.

Wasting no time, a few minutes later, I reached his apartment. I knocked on his door, stomach growling, and my mind still juggling job applications.

As he opened the door, I dropped my bag and settled in.

I was expecting my friend to prepare the usual evening meal at this time of the hour. Instead, there he was—staring at his laptop like it held the secrets of the universe. Spoiler: it didn't.

"What's up? Dinner time?" I joked, half-hoping for food.

He looked up, grinning. "Have you heard of Bitcoin?"

I blinked. "Bitcoin? No... what's that?"

"I don't know much either," he admitted, "I heard it's a smart investment though."

That got my attention. With no job and no money in sight, this sounded worth discussing.

"Is it some kind of stock?"

"No", my friend replied.

"Similar to bonds or commodities like Gold and Silver."

"No, No, No. None of that. This is something different."

"Would you please reveal the suspense now and tell more about it?" I frustratingly asked as my patience began to wear thin.

"It's not like stocks or bonds. It's digital money—no company, no government behind it. I remember back in the days, people used to get Bitcoin by solving puzzles. There was a weird name for this process. Let me recollect.

What was it...What was it...Ahh, yes – They called it mining."

"Mining?" Hmmmm. "How much was Bitcoin worth back then?"

"Maybe a dollar or so."

"And now?" I casually asked, certainly not expecting what he was about to reveal next.

That notorious smile on his face as he spoke. "Around $650."

My mind froze for a second. I asked again just to be 100% sure I heard it right.

"Did you say $650?"

"Yes, yes." He laughed. "Crazy, right?"

"So it went from $1 to $650 in less than a decade? How is that possible?"

"I know. Sounds almost too good to be true, right?"

"Yeah, that's insane. And you said people got it for free by mining?"

"Yes, that's what I remember," my friend confirmed.

"So why don't we learn this so-called 'mining' and start solving puzzles?" I enquired.

"Yeah. But now mining requires expensive machines. Those early days are gone."

"So, we missed out." I sighed, feeling disappointed and sad.

"Maybe we didn't," my friend began to explain.

"Think about this. How many people would know about this thing right now? Less than 1% of the population?"

That made me pause and ponder. "Well, you have a point here. Most people I know have never heard of Bitcoin. None of my friends or family members has ever brought up this topic in any kind of conversation."

"Same sentiments. Hardly anyone that I know ever talks about it."

"That's interesting. So, we are still very early in discovering this new investment."

"Exactly my point", as my friend came up with that nice cheeky smile filled with optimism.

Not getting into more details, I jumped to the question that mattered the most.

"Well, how do we buy it?" I asked.

"There's this website—Coinbase. We can buy it there."

"Still $650?" I asked nervously.

"I checked a while back, and it was close to that. Let me check the latest price. Give me 1 second."

"Oh gosh, it just hit $780," he screamed. We'd better act fast now.

We looked at each other. Two broke college grads, barely scraping by, now staring at something that felt like a golden opportunity.

Dinner was forgotten; the real feast was this opportunity. Hunger could wait, but a chance like this doesn't knock twice.

"Let's do it?" I asked.

He nodded.

"How much money do you plan to put in?" my friend asked.

"$1 million should suffice?" I casually joked.

In no time, we were unlocking our bank accounts to see how much we could afford to buy. It's worthwhile remembering that we were college grads back then and had no other source of income than our 20-hour per week part-time job, which barely made up for our house rent. In short, we were broke, and hence cared about every dollar sitting in our bank accounts.

"Alright, looks like I have some capital to invest," my friend confirmed.

"Great! I think I can pitch in some too," I responded, thrilled.

"Done deal. Let's go for it!" we confirmed with a decisive nod.

And thus, with modest funds but sky-high optimism, we grabbed our laptops and headed to Coinbase.

Ready to hit the "Buy" button and boom! Order confirmed.

"That was quick and easy," I echoed.

Little did I know that this wasn't just a small moment that happened one night. It was the beginning of something bigger for me. I closed my laptop, feeling a strange mix of excitement and fear.

My friend and I shook hands, shared a quick smile, and went back to the usual grind—scrolling job boards and sending out resumes.

As I headed back home, the thrill slowly started to fade, and doubts began to creep in.

What if I just threw away my hard-earned money? I am yet to find a job and have exhausted all my leftover money on Bitcoin. What if it's a scam? What if I regret my decision tomorrow?

I couldn't sleep that night. My mind kept circling back to that decision. Yet deep down, something told me to hang on to it and stay patient.

That night didn't just introduce me to Bitcoin.

It introduced me to an entirely new world.

A world I'm still exploring.

A world that led to this very book.

And it taught me a simple truth: sometimes the most important meals don't happen at a table. They happen in a quiet room, with a new idea—and the guts to click "Buy".

So, let's rewind to that cold winter evening in College Station, Texas: As I turned off the lights, my head buzzed with questions, and a new journey quietly began.

2

"Bitcoin or Vegas? The Gamble of a Lifetime"

A week after that special night, Texas woke up cold and quiet. I rolled out of bed and walked to the kitchen to prepare my breakfast and kick off the day.

Fully awake and settled now, I sat down at my desk, opened my laptop, and started my usual routine: job applications, resume uploads, and hoping for callbacks.

Hours passed. My shoulders ached, and so I leaned back to take a break before resuming the drill.

That's when a thought popped into my head: **"Wait… didn't I buy some Bitcoin not long ago? Let me check how that's doing."**

I opened my laptop again and logged in. There it was—Bitcoin. Rising.

A smile tugged at the corners of my mouth. That rare, fleeting feeling of pride and joy. Finally, something to celebrate on an otherwise uneventful day.

But as the numbers kept climbing, so did my anxiety.

Why is it rising so fast?

Is this a bubble? A scam? A pump-and-dump waiting to crash?

Should I sell now and lock in the profits?

My mind spiraled into a storm of doubt. The excitement quickly gave way to restlessness. But even in that chaos, something held me back from hitting the "Sell" button. A quiet instinct. A whisper of curiosity.

And just that moment, another thought hit me:

"The Professor." Yes, it's The Professor! Here's my answer.

Who was "The Professor"? He was one of the smartest teachers I knew in college, and if there was anyone whose lecture I wouldn't want to miss, that surely was his.

"The Professor would definitely know more about Bitcoin. I can simply pick his smart brain for valuable advice. Why didn't it occur to me before?" I muttered to myself, shaking my head in disbelief – "Idiot."

Fueled by a sudden burst of hope, I rushed downstairs, grabbed my bicycle, and pedaled toward my campus. Halfway there, reality hit me—

Wait. Will he be available at this time? He might not even be in college today. I slowed down, pulled out my phone, and checked his calendar. As expected, no luck.

"Let me quickly book the appointment." And so I did.

Mere confirmation that I will get to meet The Professor in just a few days was enough to pacify me for the time being. I felt much more relaxed and could sleep better now. The world wouldn't change overnight… right?

Days passed, and finally, the appointment day was here.

Excited as I could be, I showed up early, dressed a little better than usual.

After days of waiting, I was finally here. This was my chance to clear the fog, to get real answers to all the questions that had been swirling in my head.

And there he was. The Professor arrived. I stood and greeted him with a smile.

"Hey Professor."

"Hello! How are you doing?"

"Doing well, sir. It's a quiet winter day—can't complain."

He smiled. "So, what brings you here today?"

I hesitated for a bit, then said:

"Well, it's not exactly academic. I am here for some financial advice. Of late, I've been hearing a lot about Bitcoin and was curious to hear your thoughts—do you think it's a good investment for the future?"

He paused for a brief second and then came up with a one-liner that pretty much summed up his views on it:

"Listen, I'd rather go to Vegas, throw $100 at a casino, and try my luck there than invest in Bitcoin."

My heart sank. For a moment, my mind went completely blank. What the professor just said was the exact opposite of what I came to hear.

Not ready to give up just yet, I asked the same question in a slightly different way—hoping this time I'd get a more encouraging answer.

"So… are you saying I should do more research before investing?"

He nodded. "For the technology, yes. The tech could have several benefits. But Bitcoin? I wouldn't put a penny in it. It's unproven and unregulated. The idea of creating digital money out of thin air doesn't really fly."

The Professor then came up with a counter question I feared. "Have you invested some money in it?"

"No, no, Professor. Just curious. I was initially thinking of putting in a few dollars, but then I thought of consulting with you first, and I'm glad I did."

I lied.

What else could I have done? When your investment has been labeled worse than gambling, admitting the truth felt like an impossible task. No way I was going to let the professor know that the train had already left the station.

"You made a wise decision not to invest," The Professor continued.

"As I said, to me this whole thing looks fishy. If I were you, I would stay away from it." And with that, The Professor put his final stamp of rejection on Bitcoin.

"Anything else I can help you with?" The Professor asked.

"No, I am good for now, sir! Thank you very much for your time and valuable advice."

And that's how the meeting concluded.

"Holy crap. This was the worst meeting ever. Wish I had never booked the appointment," my emotions came rushing out.

Dejected and low, as I pedaled back. The words from The Professor echoed:

"I'd rather go to Vegas than..."

"Oh God." I was torn. "I waited for days to hear this from the professor? He just labeled my investment as gambling?"

Heartbroken and disappointed, I had run out of options. By the time I got home, I'd thus made my decision: I would sell my Bitcoin. Take the profits. Walk away.

Deep down, still, something felt off. My instincts whispered: *Stay.*

Fear shouted louder: *What if he's right? What if you lose it all?*

In the end, fear won.

"I'm going to sell and be done for good."

And on that note, I closed the chapter.

Or so I thought.

3

Unboxing Crypto: What, Why, and Who

Welcome to a new chapter. This part of the book is where we start to decipher "Digital Assets or so-called Crypto".

Until I met The Professor, I felt happy to invest in this new, well-performing asset. However, the concerning part was that my box of knowledge around crypto was dry and empty.

Not understanding this space one bit, it was obvious that anxiety and fear were my uninvited guests that would show up every now and then.

But wait. Wasn't I supposed to sell my Bitcoin and be done with it post my meeting with The Professor?

Let's rewind to where we left off.

The Missed Sale That Changed Everything

In the days after my meeting with The Professor, life got unexpectedly busy.

Selling my Bitcoin was still on my to-do list, but job hunting and other duties kept me so busy that Bitcoin took a back seat for a while until one day, it hit me like a bolt of lightning.

"Oh no. Holy crap—I didn't sell my BTC yet!"

Frustration surged through me. I scolded myself, slammed open my laptop, and readied myself to finally get it over with.

As I turn on my laptop and the screen loads, what do I notice?

Bitcoin was going up. Again.

Not down. Up.

My anger instantly flipped to joy. I couldn't believe my luck. I silently thanked the chaos of the last few days for distracting me from selling too soon.

And in that moment, something shifted inside me. The curious, entrepreneurial side of me woke up.

"Wait a second… I'm not selling this. I'm diving in."

I wanted to understand what this thing really was. Why does it exist? What problem does it solve? Who created it? I want to know everything about this new asset.

It was time to put my business degree to work and begin my Bitcoin investigation.

To understand what I was holding, I started asking questions. It was time to open this black box wide open and see what really lay inside.

Out came my laptop as I began to Google.

Q1: What is Cryptocurrency?

A: Cryptocurrency is a form of virtual money that relies on cryptography for security and operates on a decentralized technology called **Blockchain**.

Great start! None of this makes sense to me. Cryptography? Decentralized technology? Way too confusing.

To help me out, the internet broke the word 'Cryptocurrency' into two parts: 'Crypto' + 'Currency'.

- **Crypto** → short for *cryptography*, the science of securing information.
- **Currency** → something that can be used as a medium of exchange.

Ok. Fine. But what is it? More curiosity popped up in the form of the following questions:

- *"Currency? Isn't it something created and managed by the governments and banks?"*
- *"And what in the world does this 'virtual' mean? Is it not real?"*

The internet responded:

"Yes, traditional currencies are indeed managed by central banks. But cryptocurrencies are different—they're not controlled by any government or banks."

Hmm, that doesn't sound comforting. If Crypto is not created by the governments or central banks, can anyone create it? My friends, my neighbors, or I myself?

For the time being, I chose to accept the unsatisfactory answer that was on offer and moved on.

I next began to seek an explanation for the whole "Virtual" definition. This is what I uncovered – "Virtual" means it exists digitally, not in physical form like coins or notes. You can't physically touch or hold it, but that doesn't make it worthless. Its value comes from scarcity, usefulness, and trust in the system.

Think of it this way: When you pay for a Netflix subscription, you never see physical cash—you just use digital money. Bitcoin works on a similar concept, except it's not tied to any bank or country.

It honestly took me months to come to terms with such weird definitions before I finally made peace with them.

For now, moving to the next question seemed like a wise thing to do.

Q1: What is Bitcoin?

A: It's a cryptocurrency.

Digital money powered by blockchain technology. The word Bitcoin combines bit (a unit of digital information) and coin (a unit of money)

Ok, that confirms it. Bitcoin is a cryptocurrency. Fine. Let's keep rolling.

Q2: When did Bitcoin launch?

A: 2009.

"Wow, has it really been that long? That's hard to believe."

Q3: Who created it?

A: Satoshi Nakamoto.

I curiously tried searching for his picture until I gave up. In addition, there was no background information or other relevant details about this person. Just a name. A mysterious figure. No clue why.

Q4: Where's the office?

A: There isn't one.

Q5: Any support team or contact info?

A: None.

I paused.

Hang on for a moment. A digital currency… without a company, office, or support team? Faceless creator, too?

Red flag. Definitely a big red flag. How could this even be possible?

Now I understood why The Professor was skeptical. If something went wrong, who would I call?

First that weird Crypto definition, and now this.

Shaking my head in disbelief, I still pressed on to my next question.

Q6: How is Bitcoin created?

A: Bitcoins are created through a process called mining. Blockchain is the technology behind it.

"Let me read more about this technology," I instructed myself. And so, I dove in.

Thousands of miners globally compete to solve a very hard math puzzle. The first miner to solve the puzzle adds the block to the blockchain and earns New Bitcoins, and this is how Bitcoins are continuously created.

Let's better understand this important concept of "**Mining**" with the help of an example.

Lock and Key Challenge

- There's a magical lock that only opens with a key that fits perfectly.
- You don't know what the key looks like, so you keep making keys and trying them.
- After millions of tries, one key finally works!
- You open the lock, add your name to the treasure chest, and get **gold coins (Bitcoin)** as a reward.

To my easement, the technology was indeed powerful.

There was actual science and engineering behind Bitcoin. A sigh of relief!!!

"Finally!" I screamed from within.

"My first satisfactory answer." This was the first time in my investigation journey that I felt happy and at ease.

Time for the Big Question.

Q7: What problem does Bitcoin solve?

This was my make-or-break moment. If Bitcoin was a real deal, it had to solve real problems. "There better be a good answer to this one", I prayed as the screen started to load.

The explanation thesis began.

1. **You're in charge of your money.**

   After the 2008 financial crisis, trust in banks evaporated. People lost homes, savings, and hopes. Bitcoin emerged as an alternative—a system where you control your money, not a bank. No middlemen. No gatekeepers.

2. **It's for everyone.**

   Billions still lack basic banking access. Bitcoin doesn't discriminate. If you have a phone and internet, you can participate. True financial inclusion. In a world where the rich have access to everything and the poor are often left knocking on closed doors, this sounded like a level playing field for all.

3. **Radical transparency.**

   Traditional banking is a black box. We don't know what happens behind the scenes. Bitcoin is an open book—anyone can see how many coins exist, where they are, and how they move. Yet your identity stays private. Transparent and secure.

4. Fast and cheap transfers.

As an international student, I knew the pain of sending money across borders via banks. Money transfers were slow, expensive, and unpredictable—sometimes taking a week or more. In a world where information moves instantly, this felt outdated.

Bitcoin flipped that on its head. With just a wallet address, I could send money anywhere in under an hour for a little fee. No middlemen, no delays. It was simple—and honestly, mind-blowing.

(Quick note: In crypto, your "account" is called a "wallet." Same idea, different name.)

5. Scarcity vs. Abundance: The Case for Bitcoin.

Let's talk about scarcity—a concept Bitcoin is built on.

As we have experienced over the decades, Fiat money is Abundant and Inflationary. Governments print money at will to stimulate growth – a process nowadays called with a fancy term – Quantitative Easing.

Well, what does that lead to? More money, rising inflation. And what does that result in? It erodes the value of money. It erodes the purchasing power of the common man and the poor. A vicious cycle with a never-ending solution.

Bitcoin was different. It came with a limited supply. Only 21 million Bitcoins will ever exist.

Now, let's contrast it with fiat currency, which loses value constantly.

For example, if I have ₹10 million Indian Rupees in 2017, that would be worth around ₹2 million in 30 years, assuming a modest

5% inflation. Talk about "**Ethical Robbying**" and why people keep worrying about "How to grow my money" all the time.

Having spent a few hours decoding this world, I chose to pause here for a bit to digest what I just read and if it made sense to me.

"Yes. These all sound like real problems that exist."

"Yes, the current system feels slow, and the idea of Bitcoin's limited supply does sound promising."

Slowly but surely, I started to resonate with all the above points except the fact that while we can't trust banks, can we trust this whole "math-driven technology" to keep our money safe?

"Most questions answered. Thank you, Google. Just this last one for you."

Q8: Why 21 million Bitcoin? What's the magic behind this number?

A8: Google responded with a math-heavy answer involving block rewards and halving cycles.

Here's how I understood it:

Bitcoin needed a fixed supply number that worked with its reward system.

In my view, that number could have been 2.1 million, 21 million, or 210 million—as long as it would fit the system's logic. A number that would balance between scarcity and usability.

21 million was maybe one of the sweet spots Satoshi ended up picking. Enough to make Bitcoin valuable, but not so rare that it'd be impractical globally.

"Wow! There's so much that I learned today. This research exercise was pretty useful."

"I now know this asset much better and can comfortably talk about it."

I can even educate others around Bitcoin, including, guess who? The Professor. He may be a smart and knowledgeable guy, but maybe he overlooked Bitcoin? Maybe he never had the time to dive this deep into the topic, and hence doesn't realize its benefits as I do?

"Anyways, let's pack up now and wrap up the Bitcoin Deep Dive."

That night, I didn't just learn about Bitcoin—I felt its potential. What started as a plan to sell turned into a mission to understand.

And that curiosity shaped my journey in ways I couldn't imagine.

This wasn't a detour.

This was the beginning of something much bigger.

Just as I was about to close the research doors, a revelation emerged: Bitcoin isn't alone. Something else waits in the shadows.

Let's turn the page, where the hidden players finally reveal themselves.

4

The Altcoin Era – Discovering Crypto's New Frontiers

"You make your plans, but life often has a new script ready."

Assuming Bitcoin as the "Be-All and End-All", I was all but ready to conclude the exploratory journey.

Until I noted something interesting one day.

"Ethereum, Litecoin, XRP… Oh mine. These are new names. Never heard of these before. Where did they come from? Interesting."

The new entrants smiled and waved their hands to greet me – "Hello there. We are here too. Would you like to meet us, friend?"

"Ahaaa. Looks like Bitcoin isn't alone. It now has company. New players seemed to be entering the scene."

Who are these newcomers? What is life beyond Bitcoin?

A new mission was calling—to explore these newcomers.

It was time to host a proper meet-and-greet party with the new players—and there was a compelling reason behind it.

Yes, Bitcoin remained the most famous and dominant digital asset, but there was one big barrier that stood in its way for the average person: its **price**.

Even back in 2017, Bitcoin was trading at levels that felt out of reach—especially when compared to tech giant stocks like Apple, Meta (formerly Facebook), or Microsoft. For something still so new and unheard of, it was fair to say that Bitcoin felt expensive.

Sure, you could buy fractions of a Bitcoin, but let's be honest—the human mind prefers whole numbers over decimals.

That's when Altcoins felt like the budget-friendly heroes of the crypto world. As Bitcoin was sitting on its throne with a price tag beyond reach, these contenders were trading for pennies.

For someone like me, it was like spotting a "**70% off Burger Deal**" when everyone else was dining at a five-star steakhouse. Altcoins were affordable, satisfying, and still part of the crypto experience.

The rise of alternatives such as Ethereum, Litecoin, and XRP felt like a breath of fresh air.

And now that I was much more comfortable and familiar with the space, it was easy to quickly jump in and explore why these new players were gaining traction. What value did they bring to the table compared to Bitcoin?

My research led to discovering that each coin offered something unique:

Ethereum, for example, introduced a game-changing concept: **smart contracts**.

What's a smart contract? Let's understand with the help of an example.

Imagine the case of automated loan approvals. Instead of banks and humans managing loan approval and disbursement processes, we can have an automated system that will check all the same things that a bank does, and if all is good, then the loan approval and transfer are automatically done. No banks or middlemen needed.

Let's take another example.

You agree to buy a digital artwork for $100. The smart contract says: If $100 is received, transfer the artwork to the buyer. Once you send the money, the contract executes instantly, and the artwork is successfully transferred to the buyer.

Hence, smart contracts, in simple terms, mean doing an automated job once certain conditions are met. We only touched upon a few use cases, but the examples go far beyond.

Coming from an IT background, this powerful feature immediately clicked with me. And guess what? This was a feature that Bitcoin didn't offer.

Similarly, let's briefly touch upon some other interesting coins that I met.

- XRP was built to target a trillion-dollar problem: slow, costly cross-border payments. Think of being able to send money to anyone, anytime, in seconds.
- Litecoin presented itself as the "digital silver" to Bitcoin's "digital gold" tag, as it offered faster transaction speeds and lower fees.

These weren't just cheaper alternatives—they were innovative solutions tackling real-world challenges. And slowly, this space started to grow and evolve.

Besides lower price and unique features, there was one extremely important feature that these coins offered, which Bitcoin just couldn't.

What is it?

Unlike Bitcoin's mysterious creator, Satoshi Nakamoto—a ghostly figure who vanished—these new projects had real humans leading them. Actual companies, teams, and CEOs who showed up at conferences, gave interviews, and posted roadmaps. That transparency built trust.

Bitcoin, on the flip side, clung to its enigmatic origin story, with Satoshi as its silent guardian—absent, yet forever present. You can only hope he might return someday, but don't hold your breath.

For newcomers like me, this was reassuring. More tangible, more accountable coins—something Bitcoin lacked.

As I met these new coins, I also discovered that these new names were swept into a category termed **Altcoins**. In the crypto world, anything that isn't Bitcoin falls into the Altcoin label.

Seeing this evolving space, I decided to diversify my portfolio and allocate a small portion of capital to a few Altcoins.

As they say, "Don't put all your eggs in one basket", a piece of financial advice that never goes out of fashion.

Around this very time, I also stumbled upon an intriguing and special coin: USDT.

Why special? Because it was immovable. Like a rock-solid mountain unaffected by the winds. Every time I would look at its price, it would remain stagnant.

Unlike BTC, ETH, or other coins dancing up and down every time, USDT stood still.

One USDT equaled one US dollar. Every time. No surprises. No sudden dips.

"Hmm...I don't get it. If the price is always constant, what's the point? Why does this thing even exist?" Curious, I dug in to understand why.

And this curiosity led me to unlock a new chapter in my crypto education: **Stablecoin**.

As the name suggests, a stablecoin has a stable value.

1 USDT was always equal to 1 dollar. In layman's terms, it's fair to say that USDT was the digital or virtual version of the US Dollar. Hence the name: stablecoin. Clever, right?

"Ok, I get it. It's a stable value. I still don't understand what problem it solves, though?" Why would people invest in it?

To my surprise, the benefits were several. Here we go.

Price Stability

Imagine you're at a casino playing poker. The market is the poker table—chips flying, bets rising, emotions high. Suddenly, the game gets wild, and you don't want to risk losing everything.

Instead of leaving the casino (selling all your crypto and cashing out), you simply move your chips to a safe corner—a stablecoin like USDT or USDC. These coins are pegged to the U.S. dollar, so their value doesn't swing like Bitcoin or Ethereum.

When the chaos settles and you're ready to play again, you can bring your chips back to the table.

In short:

- Crypto market = poker table
- Stablecoins = safe corner for your chips
- You = player avoiding the storm without leaving the game

Medium of Exchange

Imagine you want to send your friend $100 worth of crypto. If you choose Bitcoin or Ethereum, their prices can swing wildly—even in minutes. So, by the time your friend receives it, that $100 could be $95 or $110.

With stablecoins like USDT or USDC, the value is pegged to the U.S. dollar. So, if you send $100 in USDC, your friend gets exactly $100 in USDC—no surprise dips or spikes during the transfer.

Example:

- You owe your friend $100 for dinner.
- You send 100 USDC (each worth $1).
- They receive 100 USDC, which equals $100—no volatility, no drama.

It's like sending digital dollars instantly, without worrying about the crypto rollercoaster.

Stablecoins brought calm to the crypto storm. They weren't here to make quick fortunes—they were here to protect what you already owned.

So, the crypto world wasn't just "Bitcoin vs Altcoins."

We now discovered another category – "Stablecoins vs non-stablecoins."

- Non-stablecoins: for those chasing gains.
- Stablecoins: for those preserving sanity.

At this point, building my crypto knowledge felt easier than landing a job as a foreign national in the U.S.

Having said that, despite my growing interest, crypto was still a side hustle. My main goal hadn't changed, and that was to find a job.

The crypto ride was thrilling, but the excitement never lasted long. Most of my days were still consumed by studying, sending out applications, worrying, and whispering silent prayers for a job.

Time slipped through my fingers. And before I knew it, my last day of college had arrived. The graduation I had dreamed of—celebrating with my parents—never happened.

Still holding on to my American Dream, I kept moving. Chasing opportunities from San Antonio to Austin, then Tampa, and finally North Carolina. Those days were brutal—filled with uncertainty, exhaustion, and doubt.

And then, just when my patience was wearing thin, the universe answered.

I landed a job in the U.S.

That feeling… those emotions… they're hard to put into words. It was as if I had conquered the world.

"And this little part of my life… this special part of my life… is called Happiness."

5

Greed, Hype, and the ICO Gold Rush

We've just wrapped up the thrill of Altcoins and the calm of stablecoins—the shiny new frontiers of crypto.

And to top it all off, I had landed my first job in the States. A dream came true.

What more could I have asked for? I was filled with joy and couldn't be happier. Everything was starting to fall in place. Life felt stable, and the future felt predictable.

But stability in crypto? That's a myth. Beneath the surface, there's always something cooking.

Welcome. Welcome to a new chapter, where we step off the bright, shiny path and now venture into the dark and shadowy side of crypto.

Little did I know, this wasn't just the next frontier—it was a gold rush fueled by greed and hype, as I was busy taking notes.

And so, it begins.

In 2017, I moved to Tampa, Florida.

It was time to kickstart my IT career in the U.S.

The Sunshine State welcomed me with open arms—gorgeous weather, stunning beaches, and the cherry on top: no state tax.

Everything I had hoped for and more.

Often called the "Epicenter of Entertainment," Florida's vibe made me feel like life was finally settling into place.

But isn't that the thing about life? Just when you think you've settled, a shake-up is waiting right at the front door.

The introduction of Altcoins brought a whole new wave of tokens.

Well, first it became harder—and then nearly impossible for me to keep up.

Before I could finish my research on this new token that just launched yesterday, a few more were waiting in the queue for their turn.

Next week, a few more.

What? How?

Where's this flood of uninvited guests coming from?

To add to that, each token claimed to be the next big thing.

The space wasn't just growing; it was exploding, and staying on top of it felt like chasing a hurricane with a paper map.

Some were dreamers, inspired by the promise of decentralization and financial freedom.

But many were schemers, drawn in by the lure of easy money. This very phase marked the birth of a new trend.

A trend sweeping the crypto world: **Initial Coin Offerings, or ICOs**.

Think of ICOs as the crypto version of IPOs (Initial Public Offerings) in traditional finance—but with one major difference: No regulation. No due diligence. No accountability.

As curiosity took over, my investigation revealed that most such projects banked upon Ethereum's powerful smart contract technology.

Launching a new cryptocurrency became as easy as starting a blog.

And the script to pump a token wasn't that complex. All you needed was:

- A whitepaper (which could be copied or stuffed with buzzwords),
- A flashy website (preferably with a countdown and roadmap),
- Some celebrity tweets or influencer shoutouts,
- And a lively Telegram group filled with hype.

Boom. You were ready to raise millions.

The market flooded with new tokens, most promising to revolutionize industries they barely understood. From "AI-powered decentralized dating apps" to "blockchain-based banana supply chains," the ideas were endless—and often downright absurd.

Logic didn't matter. Greed took over.

Retail investors threw money at anything with a token and a ticker. Many didn't even read the whitepapers. They just wanted to get in before the next 10x, 100x, or 1000x.

The worst part? Some scam projects outperformed legitimate ones. Shocking as it sounds.

A few overnight millionaires, a handful of viral success stories, and suddenly, everyone wanted a slice of the pie.

"Why bet on a slow horse when you can ride a rocket?"

The mood had shifted. From curiosity to mania. From innovation to speculation.

This was crypto's dark chapter—a gold rush where the only thing more abundant than tokens was human greed.

"Wait a second. What's going on here? Never had I witnessed such a level of craze and hype." It felt surreal, almost impossible to digest. None of the lessons from my business degree applied here.

Why on earth were these ICO tokens pumping so much? None seem to be solving a real-world problem? What's driving such crazy profits and prizes?

Is this even legal, and should it be allowed to happen?

And where were the regulators? Nowhere.

The whole space operated in a legal gray zone. Billions poured in, often to projects with no product, no team, and no plan—just promises and hype.

It was like a movie robbery in broad daylight, with the cops stuck in traffic.

"Regulators will arrive," people said. "Eventually."

But by then, the damage was done.

What fascinated me wasn't just the scams—it was how easily people fell for them.

And this is the part where I too raise my hand and plead guilty. I wasn't immune. A small chunk of my paycheck found its way into the ICO frenzy during those early days.

Why? For two good reasons.

First, I didn't want to miss out on what looked like a rocket taking off—a trend everyone was talking about.

Second, back then, peeling back the layers of what was happening behind the scenes felt like trying to crack a secret code written in an alien language.

Remember, this was 2017, not 2026. The rules were unwritten, the space was wild, and the future felt limitless. So, in 2026, it might sound like "How could you have fallen for this?" but back in the days, it seemed like a bold, viable move. A chance to be part of something revolutionary.

That ICO investment? It now sits perfectly in my "Lessons Learned diary"—the very lessons I'm sharing with you in this chapter.

The ICO craze was more than just token sales. It reflected what happens when unchecked ambition meets unregulated opportunity.

A time when:

- Whitepapers replaced business plans.
- Telegram groups replaced investor meetings.
- Hype replaced fundamentals.

The boom was a double-edged sword.

It brought capital, talent, and attention—but also scams, losses, and broken dreams.

It revealed the power of decentralized fundraising. But also, the dangers of a system without checks and balances.

Watching these events unfold, one thing was clear: Crypto had to grow up. Or else?

Let's flip the page and step into the heart of the frenzy.

6
The Crash

Welcome reader. Welcome to a new chapter.

Florida is a dream in the fall season. The sticky summer heat finally loosens its grip, the air turns crisp, and the sun feels like a warm hug instead of a furnace.

I was having a good time at work and outside of it. The view from my office was epic—you could watch dolphins jumping around in the waves right outside.

With the new job also came new people in life—colleagues, friends, neighbors.

And with those new connections, one topic kept coming up: Bitcoin. Crypto. Ethereum. Litecoin.

Surprisingly, it wasn't me who would bring up the crypto topic. It was others.

"Hey, I bought some BTC today." "Thinking of putting money into Litecoin." "Ethereum's looking solid."

These weren't hushed whispers anymore. These were vibrant conversations—in offices, coffee shops, weekend hangouts—especially among people in their 20s and 30s. There was a buzz, a belief, a boldness. Everyone wanted a ticket to the Crypto Kingdom.

Hence, even though the ICO Red flag that we just uncovered in the previous chapter did raise a few eyebrows, most still didn't care as long as money was to be made.

Back in India too, I heard similar stories. Friends, cousins, neighbors—began to take note of Crypto. Meanwhile, China quietly became the mining capital of the world, leveraging cheap electricity and low hardware costs to dominate Bitcoin production.

Crypto was slowly spreading its wings everywhere.

That said, not everyone was cheering.

This is us living in the year 2017. A time when governments across the world—India, China, the U.S.—were generally cautious, even hostile. Crypto was a gray area, and only a few authorities were willing to embrace it.

Often, I would come across the headlines "India Considers Ban on Crypto Trading" or "China Cracks Down on Mining".

Financial institutions weren't welcoming either. And honestly, they weren't wrong.

At that time, the headaches outweighed the promise that the crypto industry had to offer. The tech was raw. Scams were rampant. Volatility was hair-raising.

But here's the twist—the everyday person didn't care. It was the people—not the institutions—leading this charge. Crypto was born from the grassroots, and it was growing fast.

As the months rolled by, autumn faded, and winter quietly took its place.

A nice transition from the beautiful fall season to that nice breeze of cold air that you otherwise don't get to experience in the Sunny state. Holiday lights began to glow, celebrations were in full swing, and vacation mode was calling.

On a personal note, I was counting days to board my flight back to India—to my roots, my family, my home.

This trip felt different. The hustle of college was behind me. I had a job and life was good.

As I flew across continents, crypto was hitting warp speed. The market had shifted from second to fifth gear in a matter of weeks. New investors poured in like there was no tomorrow.

Gains weren't just big—they were unreal. Not 10%, not 20%, but 100%+ in a day.

It was every investor's dream.

Stocks? Mutual funds? Too slow, too boring. Crypto was the new gold rush.

For the first time, I stumbled upon a phrase that seemed to define the frenzy of the moment: FOMO—Fear of Missing Out.

People mortgaged their homes, maxed out credit cards, borrowed from friends—all to ride the crypto wave.

As the tide was rising, so was my confidence in this asset by an equal measure.

I thus convinced my brother to hurry and join the party before it gets too late. Worried and skeptical, he still chose to join the ride as he had faith in my knowledge and wisdom, and the price charts were simply too attractive to ignore.

In a matter of days, my brother's portfolio started climbing. Watching his investment grow so quickly lit up his face with excitement—and honestly, I felt proud too. Proud to play the role of the family's go-to financial advisor.

In the blink of an eye, 2017 became a memory to cherish, and the promise of a new year unfolded before us.

With bags packed and tickets in hand, Dad and Mom were all set to join me on my return to the U.S. as vacation time ended.

This was Mom and Dad's first trip to the States, and I couldn't be more excited to show them around this amazing country that had so much to offer in terms of beauty, culture, and entertainment.

Interestingly, as the calendar flipped from 2017 to 2018, so did crypto's fortunes.

For the first time, the charts began to show a clear downward trend. Sure, there had been dips before—but they were short-lived, just tiny bumps on an otherwise steep climb. This time felt different. The red candles weren't fading. They were multiplying.

I brushed it off: *'Just a healthy correction. Happens in every market. No big deal.'* With that mindset, I buried myself in office work, still holding faith in digital assets.

Yet, as the days slipped by, the market clung stubbornly to its downward course.

Still, I held to my conviction that the tide would turn—any day now—and so I waited, patient and unwavering.

Days slipped into weeks, weeks into months. But the charts kept sliding lower—like a relentless slope with no end in sight.

Slowly, the painful truth finally sank in: Oh mine. This is not a harmless dip. The market had **crashed**.

Like every bubble, this one had to burst. And burst it did. The party came crashing down.

Reality hit. Because life isn't a fantasy where you can speed forever. Sooner or later, you get a ticket—or you crash.

Crypto crashed and crashed hard. Tokens bled value. Red candles filled the charts.

Portfolios were slashed by 50%, then 70%, then 90% and beyond.

Those shouting "Crypto to the moon!" were now whispering prayers for survival.

And the latecomers who joined at the peak? Completely wiped out.

A story that hits close to home, because it sadly mirrors my brother's investment journey.

I went from being the family's proud financial consultant to someone with little pride left.

Remember the ICO machine from the last chapter? It turned out not to be a token factory. It was a money-sucking machine. Once your money was in, it rarely came out.

Several projects vanished overnight. Websites disappeared and the founders went dark.

The term "rug pull" entered the crypto lexicon. As I dug deeper, studies revealed that over 80% of ICOs in 2017 were scams.

Projects like Pincoin, iFan, and Savedroid made headlines—raising millions, then disappearing without a trace.

With portfolios down by 90%, sentiment shifted. Criticism rained down.

"I told you it was a scam."

"Crypto has no value."

"It's a Ponzi scheme for tech bros."

A time when The Professor's words again began to echo in my ears, sharp and mocking, as if he was standing right in front and pointing a finger at me – *"Stay away from it. I told you so".*

Was all my research a joke?

Was this really the future of finance—or just a well-disguised trap?

For the first time, I truly understood Warren Buffett's wisdom:

"Be fearful when others are greedy."

The crypto train, once packed with passengers, was now running dry.

No new riders.

Just silence.

This was the moment I had to stop and ask myself, "What triggered this chaos? No one saw this coming?"

As I went down the memory lane, the truth hit me: the signs were there all along – "Suspicious ICOs, Unstoppable Gains, No Regulations".

And so, the honest admission came – "This wasn't bad luck. This was inevitable. And I should have seen it coming."

Watching the crash unfold was soul-crushing. I can try to put those feelings into words, but the truth is stark—the real pain could only be understood by those who lived through it.

Personally, I considered myself lucky. Crypto was never my main gig.

Did it hurt? Oh yes. It hit with the sting of a bee, but it didn't break me as my life went on with the usual 9-to-5 job.

But for many, it was devastating. Dreams shattered. Savings gone. Trust broken.

And with that, let's wind up crypto's first great crash—a chapter that didn't just make headlines but carved its place in the history books, not for the right reasons.

Down and dusted, crypto's fairy tale may have paused. But the story? Far from finished.

7

Not Your Keys, Not Your Coins – My Wake-Up Call in Crypto

At this point in my journey, I thought I had seen it all—the shady projects, fake websites, and the big crash that wiped out fortunes overnight.

I had survived the chaos, learned my lessons, and believed the worst was behind me.

I was wrong.

Another lesson was waiting. One that was scarier than anything before. And I can still picture the moment like it happened yesterday—the day that shook my entire perspective on crypto.

Up until now, I thought the hardest part in crypto was taking the leap—convincing yourself to buy those volatile coins and ride the storm. Once you are past that, it feels simple: sit back, keep your 9-to-5 routine, and let your portfolio do its thing in the background.

Easy, right?

Until the day I learned the truth:

Buying is the easy part. Owning them? That's the real challenge.

Confused? Well then, let's open the door and dive right into this new chapter as this one gets personal.

"**Your account has been compromised**."

An email that hit me like a thunderclap one day.

My stomach dropped. My hands froze on the keyboard.

The exchange where I kept my crypto—the platform I trusted—was warning me that my account might have been hacked.

The ground beneath me vanished. My heart pounded as the nightmare played out in my head: Did my coins vanish? Is everything gone?

I rushed to log in, whispering prayers between breaths as the screen loaded—each second stretching into an eternity.

And then... relief. My coins were still there. I exhaled hard, refreshing the page again and again, half-expecting the nightmare to return.

Tests confirmed it: my account was safe.

So, what was with that terrifying email?

Turns out, the breach was real—but instead of notifying only the affected users, it seemed like the exchange blasted a blanket email to pretty much every registered user.

Panic spread like wildfire. Forums exploded. People were freaking out. And I was one of them.

While I was lucky this time, the danger was real.

Keeping my money on that platform felt like playing with fire. I scrambled to move my funds to another exchange, my fingers flying across the keyboard like my life depended on it.

Only after the transfer was complete did I breathe again.

But the fear lingered.

Today, it's this exchange. Tomorrow, what if it's the new one, I just moved my digital assets to? Do I really have a choice here?

That's when the reality hit me: Even if you survive the scams and the market crashes, your assets can still vanish—because of security risks you can't control.

And here's what baffled me: Never had I heard of a stock or a mutual fund platform being hacked. So why crypto?

The answer lay in the technology—but that didn't make the reality any less unsettling.

Exchanges, Wallets, and the Illusion of Safety

As I delved deeper into the subject, I began exploring different exchanges and assessing their reliability. While platforms like Coinbase seemed more trustworthy than many others, none could truly claim to be immune from hacks.

Another limitation soon became clear: every exchange only supported a limited set of tokens. If you wanted to buy something outside that list, you had no choice but to turn to other platforms.

An important callout here – These Platforms or exchanges fell into the category of **Centralized Exchanges.** Why do we call them Centralized?

Because they are operated and controlled by a single company or entity.

But centralization came with risks. Hackers lurked everywhere, probing for weaknesses. Breaches weren't rare headlines anymore; they had become routine.

My research revealed a sobering truth: the keys to my crypto weren't in my hands at all—they were held by the exchange.

In the crypto world, there's a popular phrase that captures this perfectly: **"Not your keys, not your coins."**

That saying became my wake-up call. If I wanted real security, I needed control.

That search led me to **hardware wallets**. These physical devices, much like USB drives, allow you to transfer your crypto and then disconnect from the internet. Known as **cold wallets**, they offer two powerful advantages:

- The private key—the secret code to your funds—is yours alone.
- Once offline, your assets are shielded from online hacks.

Hardware wallets quickly became the gold standard for security. Yet they weren't flawless:

- Lose your key, and your crypto is gone forever—no resets, no support.
- Active traders found them impractical; they're built for storage, not daily trading.
- Even hardware devices weren't immune—stories of compromised units surfaced too.

Beyond centralized exchanges and hardware wallets, another option emerged: the **Decentralized Exchange (DEX)**.

Unlike centralized platforms, a DEX operates without a single authority. You hold your own keys, and trades happen directly between users through blockchain-based smart contracts. Examples include **Uniswap** and **PancakeSwap**.

Because decentralized exchanges operate without central oversight, they tend to be less regulated and more anonymous.

DEXs had other problems too.

DEXs run on smart contracts, and if those contracts contain bugs or haven't been properly audited, hackers can exploit them to drain funds. Other challenges exist too—liquidity issues, malicious tokens—all reminders that even in the world of decentralization, risks remain.

I won't dive into every detail here, but the web is full of cautionary tales for those who want to explore further.

In the end, one truth stood firm: **There was no single place to park digital assets with absolute safety.**

Security thus was, and still is, the Achilles' heel of the crypto ecosystem—a grave reason many stay away from this asset to this day.

People work tirelessly day in and day out in pursuit of earning money. Decades of Blood, sweat, and sacrifice go into building futures. Entrusting that capital to unsecured platforms and devices? That was a gamble few were willing to take, and rightly so.

Unlike banks or regulated financial institutions, crypto exchanges operated in a gray zone—no oversight, no guarantees.

Regulators? Again absent. Just like in the movies, the cops always show up late.

Sad and unfortunate!

But here's the bright side: every problem presents an opportunity.

Airplanes weren't safe on day one. Neither were elevators nor self-driving cars. Crypto had flaws—but if it offered real value, those flaws could be fixed.

But back in 2018, the bigger question still loomed:

How can this industry ever thrive—let alone gain credibility—when its flaws overshadow its potential?

Time to segway to the next chapter.

8

The Phoenix Rises

Look at that—we're halfway home and the ride's just getting fun.

We've crossed the midpoint. Thank you for being part of the journey so far.

Let's keep moving, though, as there's a lot more to unpack.

Year 2018 slowly slipped by, carrying its own share of quiet changes as 2019 arrived.

On a personal front, 2019 brought a big shift for me—as I traded the sunny beaches of Florida for the vibrant rhythm of Nashville, Tennessee, the city of music and endless energy.

Yes, a lot of people love moving places. I'm the exact opposite, though.

For me, relocating feels like a marathon of hassles—packing every last item, selling things I can't carry, reorganizing everything at the new place, and worst of all, saying goodbye to friends and a city I fell in love with.

But this time, I didn't have a choice. A new project came calling, and 'no' wasn't part of the vocabulary. So, with a heavy heart and packed suitcases, I embraced the change and hoped Nashville would have its own charm waiting for me.

What else was I hoping for? For the crypto tide to turn and turn soon.

But as they say, "Things happen when they happen."

A brief spark of promise in early 2019 faded into disappointment by year's end.

For Digital Assets, the years 2018 and 2019 felt like an endless winter—slow, heavy, and unforgiving.

What was once close to a $600 billion juggernaut in 2017 limped into 2019, barely clinging to $180 billion. Ouch.

"Bitcoin is headed to zero," declared countless financial prophets as my own confidence began to waver.

And honestly, it was hard to argue. You couldn't buy a cup of coffee with Bitcoin. You couldn't pay your rent with it. No one was using Bitcoin for Payments. In all fairness, no one was using it for anything.

And without utility, selling Bitcoin to a newbie was like selling a parachute to someone who's never been on a plane—sounds cool, but they have no idea why they need it.

Hence, it was fair to say that at that moment, there seemed to be no practical reason for Bitcoin to defend its lofty price tag.

Then came 2020.

A year that felt like crypto's final audition. Would it survive the storm or fade into the digital abyss?

Like many, I watched from the sidelines, popcorn in hand, waiting to see if this was the end or just an intermission.

And just as the curtain seemed poised to close, COVID-19 entered stage left.

Global panic, lockdowns, economic chaos—the perfect conditions for crypto to quietly disappear.

Wrong.

Despite standing on one leg, the crypto industry showed grit. Scam projects vanished while the serious builders kept building. And slowly, the tide began to turn.

🌱 Green Shoots of Recovery

Regulators finally woke up from their slumber.

After years of watching from the sidelines, they stepped in with compliance frameworks like KYC (Know Your Customer) and AML (Anti-Money Laundering). These measures didn't just add rules—they added credibility.

For the first time, the crypto space began to feel less like the Wild West and more like a marketplace with guardrails.

Along with fixing existing problems, new use cases blossomed:

- You could now lend and borrow money using crypto.
- Passive income from tokens? Yes, please.

DeFi—Decentralized Finance—was no longer just a buzzword; it was a movement.

Here's a little detour of DeFi.

In a simple one-liner: DeFi is money without middlemen, powered by code instead of banks.

You don't need a bank account, permission from humans, or a perfect financial record.

In traditional finance:

You ask a human → they check → they approve → they take their cut → then you get what you want.

In DeFi:

You press a button → the vending machine instantly gives you what you need (loan, trade, interest, etc.) → because it's programmed to.

No bank manager. No rejections because of "low credit score."

No paperwork. Just code.

In summary, DeFi (Decentralized Finance) is a system where all kinds of financial activities—saving, borrowing, trading, investing—happen without banks, brokers, or middlemen. The system runs on blockchain powered by Smart Contracts.

With that, let's return to the main narrative.

Adding feathers to its wings, Crypto slowly but surely began to add all the major elements of traditional finance and more.

💰 Big Money, Bigger Bets

Going back in time, while 2018 and 2019 were perceived as quiet and boring years, behind the scenes, big institutional players were slowly positioning themselves for this asset. Let's uncover a few such developments.

Financial giants like Fidelity launched crypto custody services in 2019—aiming to solve the "Where do I keep my coins?" dilemma.

This opened the floodgates for pension funds and hedge funds eager to dip their toes in.

Talking about Big players, 2019 was also when the giant Meta (formerly Facebook) decided to place its bet on Crypto and launch its highly ambitious digital token Libra.

Libra, unfortunately, didn't see the light of day, thanks to regulatory scrutiny and Meta already under the hammer for data scandals. But the move confirmed that big players and big money were all but ready to enter the arena.

Meanwhile, Bakkt, a platform backed by the New York Stock Exchange, launched Bitcoin futures in 2019—a huge institutional nod.

It was no longer just the common man carrying the crypto torch forward. Institutions were here to join hands and ride the ride.

With growing interest from both institutions and retail investors, the digital asset industry began expanding its features and offerings.

As the world's attention shifted toward artificial intelligence, the crypto space followed suit.

AI-powered projects such as **SingularityNET** and **Numerai** stepped into the spotlight, showcasing how machine learning and blockchain could converge to create new possibilities—from decentralized AI marketplaces to crowdsourced predictive models for financial markets.

With such good progress behind the scenes, 2020 was bound to "Not Disappoint" and so "It didn't" as came the year of **Bitcoin Halving**.

"**Bitcoin Halving**"? Let's find out what this new phenomenon means.

Bitcoin Halving is like a rule in the Bitcoin game that makes rewards smaller over time for the Bitcoin miners. This halving event happens every 4 years (or every 210,000 blocks). Here's a bit of explanation on Halving.

- When miners solve puzzles (mine blocks), they earn Bitcoin rewards.
- The reward for mining the first Bitcoin block in 2009 was 50 BTC per block.

- After the first halving in 2012, it reduced from 50 BTC → 25 BTC.
- Then → 12.5 BTC, then 6.25 BTC, and so on.
- This cycle continues until all 21 million Bitcoins are mined.

Why Does It Happen?

- To make Bitcoin scarce (like gold).
- If rewards stayed big forever, there would be too many Bitcoins.
- Halving slows down supply, which often makes Bitcoin more valuable.

Fun Examples

1. Candy Jar Game
    - You start with a jar of 50 candies.
    - Every 4 rounds, the number of candies you get for winning is cut in half.
    - Round 1: 50 candies → Round 2: 25 → Round 3: 12 → Round 4: 6.
    - Eventually, candies become super rare!
2. Treasure Hunt
    - At first, you find big gold nuggets.
    - After every few hunts, nuggets shrink to half their size.
    - By the end, you're finding tiny specks of gold.

This built-in scarcity mimics gold and makes Bitcoin a **deflationary asset**. Fewer new coins = higher demand = potential price surge. It's simple economics with a cryptographic twist.

2020 wasn't just about halving; it was about momentum.

- PayPal and Square entered the conversation.
- MicroStrategy made headlines with an aggressive Bitcoin buying spree as Michael Saylor became Bitcoin's loudest cheerleader.

Crypto was no longer a fringe experiment—it was becoming a serious asset class.

Beyond crypto, 2020 was also the year I moved back to India for good, as marriage was on the cards.

Memories of that unusual flight are still vivid—a time when COVID had gripped the world with fear and uncertainty.

It was my very first flight during the pandemic, and everything felt surreal. The aircrew greeted passengers with a sense of caution, their words muffled behind masks, reminding everyone of the invisible threat in the air.

The destination wasn't the comfort of home, but a quiet, silent hotel room where I would spend two long weeks in isolation before I could head home. Locked away, counting days, and adjusting to a new reality—it was a journey unlike any other that most of us can relate to.

🌍 2021: The Phoenix Rises

Then came 2021—and crypto didn't just recover, it exploded.

By February, Bitcoin's market cap hit $1 trillion—that's trillion with a "T." It joined the elite club alongside Apple, Amazon, and Google.

From $0.004 in 2010 to nearly $60,000 in 2021—Bitcoin's comeback was legendary. The "experts" who predicted its demise? Nowhere to be found.

Tesla jumped in with a $1.5 billion investment and flirted with accepting Bitcoin for cars. (They later backtracked, citing environmental concerns—but the impact was undeniable.)

And then the real game-changer: El Salvador. The first country to adopt Bitcoin as legal tender. The first to hold it in its national treasury. A bold move heralding a new era.

From Ashes to Ascent

Crypto had done the unthinkable.

Survived a brutal crash, regulatory uncertainty, a global pandemic, relentless skepticism—and emerged stronger.

From retail investors to institutions, from startups to sovereign nations—everyone was watching.

The Phoenix had risen.

And this time, it wasn't going anywhere. Or?

9

NFTs, Memes & the Madness of 2021

Digital pets selling for thousands of dollars. A JPEG priced at $69 million. Virtual land—untouchable, intangible—auctioned for the price of a real mansion. What was the point? Only the buyers knew.

Welcome to the beautiful chaos of 2021. A year when crypto and common sense stopped returning each other's calls.

It was a time already overflowing with upheaval. Covid returned in fresh waves as debates raged over unproven vaccinations.

The Taliban took Afghanistan. The U.S. saw the Capitol riot as Joe Biden stepped into office.

If the world was going wild, why would crypto be any different?

★ It started with JPEGs.

Not just any JPEGs—these were blockchain's way of saying, "This digital thing is yours, and only yours." Suddenly, art wasn't about brush strokes or galleries; it was about NFTs.

Let's shed some light on this buzzword – NFTs.

NFT stands for Non-Fungible Token.

- Fungible means interchangeable. A $10 bill is fungible—you can swap it with another $10 bill, and nothing changes.

The same goes for Bitcoin or Ethereum. One unit is as good as another.

- Non-Fungible means unique. Think of the Mona Lisa. You can't just swap it with another painting and call it even. It's one-of-a-kind.

So, an NFT is a unique digital asset, recorded on the blockchain, that proves ownership of something—be it digital art, music, videos, domain names, or even… tweets.

Yes, someone literally bought a tweet. Crazy right?

🖼 The $69 Million JPEG

Let's pause for a moment to admire one of the most iconic NFTs ever sold:

"Everydays: The First 5000 Days" by digital artist Beeple.

This masterpiece is a mosaic of 5,000 digital artworks created daily from May 1, 2007, to February 21, 2021. 13.5 years of daily ritual. The price tag? A jaw-dropping $69 million.

"Wait… someone paid that much for a file they can't even hang on a wall?"

Art is subjective, of course. So, you decide—what's it worth to you?

$69? $690? Or $69 million?

And yes, that's the first of two images in this book. Take a moment. Google this image and soak it in.

🐱 Then Came the Pets

Bored Apes and pixelated punks became the new status symbols. Owning a cartoon monkey wasn't just quirky—it was a badge of honor, a ticket into exclusive clubs, and sometimes, a flex worth more than a luxury car.

People weren't just buying art; they were buying identity, community, and bragging rights.

🌐 Virtual Land, Real Money

The Metaverse quickly joined the party.

Metaverse?

The Metaverse is like a huge online world where you can do almost anything—play games, meet friends, go shopping, watch movies—but instead of using a controller, you can walk around inside it using special tools like VR headsets.

Close your eyes—now you're on a sunlit island. Blink again, and you're scaling mountains. A moment later, snowflakes swirl around you. That's the magic of the virtual world.

The Metaverse became a playground for creativity and commerce. Virtual concerts, art galleries, and fashion shows blurred the line between the physical and digital worlds. For a moment, it felt like the future had arrived.

Crypto Projects like **Decentraland** and **The Sandbox** led the virtual world as they sold plots of virtual land—squares of 3D possibility—for breathtaking sums.

And why not? In a world where attention is the scarcest commodity, digital location matters.

Brands launched virtual stores; artists hosted concerts on pixel stages; communities built neighborhoods where gravity was more suggestion than law.

Buying virtual land felt like a bet on the future of presence. The pandemic had already moved coffee chats to Zoom and shopping carts to apps.

By 2021, the line between "online" and "real life" didn't blur—it dissolved. If we live on screens, then owning the screen space becomes the new frontier of real estate.

Wonder why Facebook rebranded to Meta? It was Facebook's ambition to build the Metaverse that led to this decision.

Overnight, the term Metaverse went from obscure to mainstream as big money flowed into VR headsets, immersive platforms, and virtual social spaces. Other players like Microsoft followed suit.

Meme Coins: When Crypto Got a Sense of Humor

But wait—2021 wasn't done yet. Enter another wild child of crypto: **Meme Coins**.

Now what's a meme coin?

A cryptocurrency born from internet memes, pop culture, or just plain fun.

No utility. No whitepapers.

Just vibes, community hype, and the occasional Elon Musk tweet.

"Awesome! Let's applaud another mind-boggling use case," I tell myself.

Leading the pack was Dogecoin—a coin that started as a joke in 2013. In 2021, it soared from less than $0.01 to over $0.60, fueled by Musk calling it *"the people's crypto"* and even featuring it on the Saturday Night Live show.

At its 2021 peak, Dogecoin had a market cap exceeding $80 billion—proving even memes can move markets and move them hard.

Then came another meme – Shiba Inu, the self-proclaimed *"Dogecoin Killer,"* with even crazier gains. Others like SafeMoon, MonaCoin, and Banano also made headlines—because why not?

In Feb 2021, Nyan Cat—the rainbow pop-tart cat—was sold for an astonishing price of over half a million dollars. Memes that once lived rent-free in our heads were now lounging in luxury suites on the blockchain.

Memes aren't just jokes—they're culture. Owning the original meme became a status symbol.

It was like saying, "I own a piece of internet history." And the blockchain made that ownership real.

Memes capture feelings in one image. When the world felt uncertain, memes gave us something solid—something funny. NFTs turned those laughs into assets.

You weren't just laughing—you were owning the laugh.

Why Did This Happen?

Three big reasons:

1. **Scarcity**
   NFTs made digital things rare. Humans love rare stuff—even if it's just pixels.
2. **Status**
   A Bored Ape wasn't just art—it was a badge of honor. Social signaling moved from luxury cars to profile pics.
3. **Speculation**
   Let's be honest—most people weren't buying for art. They were buying for profit. FOMO (Fear of Missing Out) turned the market into a casino.

Add pandemic boredom and a hunger for novelty—and boom! You get the perfect storm.

⚡ Tech Meets Culture

NFTs and Memes were filled with hype—but they also showed what's possible. Digital ownership means you can sell, trade, rent, or even fractionalize assets.

Artists earn royalties. Communities own their projects. Brands create loyalty programs that actually feel valuable.

The tech opened doors we didn't know existed.

What It Meant for the Future

The hype cooled down, but the idea stayed as NFTs plan to move beyond art into:

- Tickets & Memberships
- Gaming Assets
- Brand Loyalty Programs
- Digital Identity

2021 was wild, irrational, and unforgettable. It was the year pixels got price tags, memes got million-dollar bids, and ownership became programmable.

The Conclusion

NFTs, Memes, and the Metaverse introduced fresh ideas that not many saw coming.

But at the same time, the larger crypto scene quickly drifted back to its old habits—speculation and pure, unfiltered greed.

If crypto was already wild, NFTs and Meme Coins showed up yelling, "Hold my beer!"

Memes and NFTs became the poster children for hype over utility—the digital embodiment of "Let's throw logic out the window and see what happens."

Having learned my lessons the hard way, I kept my distance this time, watching the hype cycle from the sidelines instead of jumping into the frenzy.

The train was speeding again at 300 MPH.

Greed was back at its peak.

And as we all know by now, whenever the crypto world hits that level of euphoria, the next chapter practically writes itself.

10
Prison Time

We've come a long way.

From those hesitant first steps into the world of crypto—asking the "whys" and "what's"—to meeting Bitcoin and its Altcoin siblings.

We peeled back layers of innovation and chaos, and uncovered crypto's darker shadows: hacks, greed, scams.

And we've seen fortunes made overnight and vaporized just as quickly.

One key takeaway stands out: crypto is always on the move.

It's a pendulum—swinging left, right, up, down—but never still.

And as we stand here, staring at the tracks ahead, one question looms large: **Where is this crypto train headed next?** Toward breakthroughs or breakdowns? Triumphs or tragedies?

Welcome to Chapter 10, where we go deep down the rabbit hole.

The Calm Before the Storm

The air was thick with optimism in early 2022. Charts were green, influencers were screaming "to the moon," and Twitter was a carnival of rocket emojis. But here's the thing about euphoria—it blinds you.

One lesson burned into my memory from the 2018 crash: when optimism and hype hit fever pitch, caution becomes your best friend. The road ahead gets slippery, and you'd better watch your step.

Then February arrived like a thunderclap. Geopolitical tensions exploded into a full-blown conflict between Russia and Ukraine.

The world held its breath. Amid the chaos, Ukraine turned to crypto for survival—launching donation campaigns that raised millions in days.

It was unprecedented. A nation at war, funded by Crypto.

But this lifeline raised alarms. If Ukraine could bypass traditional banking systems, what stopped other nations from dodging sanctions using crypto's shadowy power?

The U.S. administration wasn't amused. Executive orders rolled out, tightening regulations and pulling crypto closer under compliance umbrellas. The honeymoon was over.

The Dominoes Begin to Fall

Then came the implosions. Esteemed crypto projects like **TerraUSD** and **LUNA** collapsed spectacularly, wiping out billions and triggering a chain reaction of insolvencies.

Crypto lending giants—**Celsius**, **Voyager**, **Three Arrows Capital**—crumbled like sandcastles in a storm, filing for bankruptcy one after another.

Investors watched their screens in disbelief as portfolios evaporated. Telegram groups turned into grief counseling sessions. Twitter was a battlefield of blame and despair.

But the worst was yet to come.

You know, one thing that keeps most people from crossing the line into illegal or outright criminal behavior is the fear of prison. What if the cops catch me? What if I end up behind bars?

But in the crypto world?

There was no such fear. No boundaries. No real consequences—at least not in the beginning.

So, let's dive into this lawless playground back in 2022.

November 2022: Crypto World's Dark Hour

Enter FTX—a name that, until then, stood for trust, innovation, and the big moment crypto had been waiting for.

At its peak, FTX wasn't just another exchange; it was the exchange. The cool, shiny platform everyone talked about. Big enough for Wall Street, simple enough for everyday traders.

Millions of users joined it. Celebrities promoted it. Entire stadiums carried its name. And at the center of it all was Sam Bankman-Fried—SBF—seen as the genius boy of modern finance. With his baggy shorts, messy hair, and "smart but shy" vibe, he became the face of crypto trust.

And then…the cracks appeared.

What came next wasn't a small money problem or a bad week in the markets. It was something much darker. The truth came out: billions of customer deposits had been secretly moved to Alameda Research, FTX's sister company, to cover risky trades and pay for a luxury lifestyle—expensive homes in the Bahamas, political donations, investments, and more.

The news hit the crypto world like a bomb. Panic spread instantly. People rushed to withdraw their money. Markets crashed. Screens turned red. And under all the pressure and unanswered questions, FTX went offline.

What followed felt like watching a crime story play out live.

In December 2022, SBF was arrested in the Bahamas, then flown to the U.S., and charged with one of the largest financial frauds ever seen. Courtrooms filled up. Headlines exploded.

By March 2024, he received a 25-year prison sentence and was ordered to give up $11 billion.

The bankruptcy process showed how bad things truly were.

John J. Ray III, the expert brought in to clean up the mess (the same man who fixed Enron), said a line that became famous:

"Never in my career have I seen such a complete failure of corporate controls and such a complete absence of trustworthy financial information."

And coming from him—that meant a lot.

The damage was massive. Hundreds of thousands of people lost their savings. Crypto markets collapsed. Whatever trust people still had was destroyed overnight.

Regulators stepped in hard. The fall of FTX became the biggest warning sign in crypto history—a painful reminder of what happens when too much power, zero rules, and greed all mix together.

The shock didn't stop with investors. The collapse triggered a chain reaction across the entire crypto space. Companies linked to FTX—lenders, trading firms, funds—started going bankrupt one after another.

Even exchanges with no connection to FTX saw customers running to pull their money out.

An industry that had spent years trying to look serious and trustworthy suddenly looked weak and unstable. Confidence disappeared. For months, even the smallest rumor caused full-blown panic.

But the biggest damage was emotional. FTX wasn't some tiny, unknown company. It was the shining star of crypto—backed by famous investors, big-name firms, celebrities, and even regulators who praised its founder.

If this could fall apart—if this was a lie—what more was hiding? Retail investors felt cheated. Big institutions slowly backed away.

Once the dust settled, one thing was clear:

The pre-FTX world—full of blind trust, excitement, and hype—was gone forever.

Crypto had seen scandals before, but nothing hit this hard, this fast, or this deep.

The Wake-Up Call

This was the moment reality finally hit. If crypto wanted to survive—let alone grow—the chaos had to stop. You can't claim to be a trillion-dollar industry at the cost of draining the savings of ordinary people right out in the open.

Wealth built on lies isn't success.

It's a ticking time bomb waiting to explode.

But here's the thing about crypto: every time the world declares it dead, it shows up at its own funeral in a Lamborghini.

Every "Crypto is over" headline is followed by reinvention, rebuilding, and rewriting the rules all over again.

With that, let's end this dark chapter of Crypto that cemented its place in the history books for all the wrong reasons.

Next, let's usher in a brighter horizon as Crypto gets its acknowledgment by the Who's Who.

Time to flip the page as we can't keep the Big Boys waiting.

11

Knock Knock!!! Wall Street is Here

How can we?

How can we talk about reshaping the financial system without confronting the very people who designed the old one?

How can we skip the giants, the pillars of traditional finance?

Welcome to a new chapter, as it's time to roll out the red carpet for the Big Boys.

From year 2016 to this far in the journey, one question always lingered in my mind.

"If and when there will come a time when the big financial giants formally say "**Yes**" to this emerging asset". Will the Big Banks and Investment Management firms ever adopt it?

BlackRock, Goldman Sachs, J.P. Morgan, and others.

If such companies publicly begin to embrace this asset, then there's definitely light at the end of the tunnel.

These are not ordinary companies we are talking about. They are names that have shaped economies, influenced governments, and set the pace of global markets for decades.

If finance were a kingdom, these firms would be the families that have always been in charge.

And let's be honest with ourselves:

Nothing monumental happens in global finance unless the "Who's Who" gives a discreet nod behind closed doors.

So, imagining a trillion-dollar crypto industry rising without Wall Street's wolves lurking at the center?

That's like trying to power a spaceship with birthday candles. It's just not happening.

By the time crypto exploded into mainstream awareness, it had already proven itself in every possible way. It had survived crashes that would've obliterated traditional industries. It had been doubted, mocked, and outlawed—and somehow it kept climbing.

Crypto wasn't fragile.

It was antifragile.

And from their glass skyscrapers, the Wall Street elites were watching all along what was at stake: not millions, not billions—but trillions of dollars.

And even more waiting on the horizon.

So, let's not assume for 1 second that the big players simply woke up one morning and said, *"Hey, crypto looks cool."*

Behind the scenes, they were watching, preparing, and positioning themselves from the very beginning.

The public embrace? Just the final act of a long and strategic play.

🎭 From Critics to Converts

Remember those CEOs who once dismissed Bitcoin?

The ones who declared, *"I'll fire anyone caught holding crypto"*?

Well, guess what? They're singing a different tune now. Suddenly, Bitcoin is *"innovative," "misunderstood," and "a valuable asset class."*

Their defense?

"We didn't understand it before. We were wrong. But now we get it."

Hard to believe, isn't it? These are some of the smartest minds in finance—and they

"didn't get" crypto while the common man did?

The only question to ask was – Why didn't Wall Street jump in much earlier?

Crypto wasn't confusing.

It was dangerous to traditional finance. A disruption sharp enough to slice through old systems.

And Wall Street doesn't like surprises.

Every industry makes an effort to protect itself from the disruptive forces. So why would Finance be any different?

Wall Street needed some time to equip itself for what was coming.

So, they bought themselves time—time to learn, adapt, build, and prepare their own versions of the future.

🕰 The Transition Begins

Once they were ready, they moved with the precision of wolves closing in on their target.

Wall Street finally understood the beauty of blockchain—not as a toy, not as a meme, but as a new backbone for money itself.

Let's uncover a few moments that cemented Wall Street's arrival.

- **January 2024**: The game-changer. The SEC approved close to a dozen **spot Bitcoin ETFs**, including giants like BlackRock and Fidelity—finally giving institutions a regulated path into crypto. This wasn't a milestone; it was a starting gun.

- **July 2024**: Ethereum took center stage. Spot Ethereum ETFs began trading on U.S. exchanges—a major win for legitimacy. Ethereum was no longer just tech—it was institutional.
- **Late 2024 into 2025**: The dominoes kept falling. Institutional adoption surged to new highs. Surveys revealed that a majority of institutional investors had already allocated capital to digital assets, with many signaling plans to expand their holdings even further.
- More ETF approvals followed as XRP, Solana, Dogecoin, and others got SEC's approval with the arrival of a more Pro-Crypto administration.
- Titan financial firms like Citi, American Express, Vanguard, Goldman Sachs, and Grayscale laid the groundwork for deeper crypto integration. Custody solutions, tokenization platforms, blockchain research—no longer tests but strategic priorities.

Firms like Grayscale describe 2026 as the "Dawn of the Institutional Era," anticipating broader access to exchange-traded crypto products, deeper integration with financial infrastructure, and the arrival of slow-moving but powerful pools of capital such as pensions and sovereign wealth funds.

Wall Street's involvement has brought credibility, liquidity, and structural depth—turning digital assets into a mainstream component of modern portfolios.

The shift wasn't just financial; it signaled a broader transformation in how global markets understand value, money, and the future of digital finance.

If there was ever a sign, this was it!!!

The Big Boys were here and the world was watching.

12

CBDCs: How Nations are Rewriting Money

Imagine this: you walk into a café, order your usual latte, and pay—not with cash or a card, but with a digital form of your national currency issued directly by the central bank. No intermediaries, no additional fees, no settlement delays. Just simple, instant payment.

Now extend that same idea to international trade. Instead of relying on slow, expensive banking networks, countries exchange value directly through interconnected digital currency systems. This isn't a futuristic concept—it's already taking shape.

This chapter goes beyond just narration. It's a win! Win for the technology and for the efficiency it provides.

If even governments find merit in blockchain, what else is left for validation?

Welcome to the era of Central Bank Digital Currencies (CBDCs), where technology and monetary policy meet to redefine how money moves.

From Concept to Reality

The idea of Central Bank Digital Currencies didn't appear out of thin air. It began gaining momentum when Bitcoin challenged long-held beliefs about what money could be and who could create it.

As cryptocurrencies grew in popularity, governments realized they needed to innovate too—on their own terms, within their own mandates.

China led the charge. Back in 2014, the People's Bank of China started developing what would eventually become the digital yuan (e-CNY). Today, its pilot spans dozens of cities and has processed billions in transactions. Soon, other nations joined the race:

- Bahamas launched the Sand Dollar in 2020—the world's first fully deployed CBDC.
- Nigeria followed with the eNaira in 2021.
- India introduced the eRupee in December 2022.

These early movers proved something important: CBDCs are no longer abstract theories or futuristic ideas—they're live systems operating in real economies, touching real people.

Why do CBDCs Matter?

CBDCs stand apart from cryptocurrencies. They're issued by the state, fully regulated, and tied directly to national currencies. Their importance lies in the real-world gaps they aim to fill.

1. **Financial Inclusion**

   In many countries, millions still lack access to formal banking. With CBDCs, anyone with a phone can hold a secure digital wallet—no branch visit, no paperwork, no minimum balance.

2. **Payment Efficiency**

   Sending money across borders often takes days and goes through several middlemen. With CBDCs, these transfers can happen in just a few seconds.

3. **Monetary Sovereignty**

   As private stablecoins and foreign payment networks expand, CBDCs allow governments to maintain control over their currency systems while still embracing innovation.

4. **Programmability**

   CBDCs can enable new possibilities: automated tax payments, targeted subsidies, transparent auditing, and compliance—features that could simplify public services.

The Global Race

Today, a majority of the world's economies—representing over 95% of global GDP—are exploring CBDCs. Progress varies:

- India's digital rupee pilot has grown steadily, seeing significant increases in both users and transaction volume.
- The European Central Bank is preparing for a digital euro with emphasis on privacy, security, and offline capability.

This isn't just a race for modernization. It's a race for geopolitical influence.

The nations that build tomorrow's digital currency infrastructure will shape global standards, financial interoperability, and trade networks for decades.

The Double-Edged Sword

Despite the advantages, CBDCs bring important considerations:

Privacy

How much visibility should governments have into individual transactions? Striking the right balance between transparency and privacy is crucial.

Cybersecurity

A national digital currency must be ultra-secure and resilient. Any vulnerability could threaten financial stability.

Questions are many, and countries are actively experimenting with what works best for their economies.

A Glimpse into Tomorrow

If current trends continue, digital forms of national currencies may gradually weave themselves into everyday life. Physical cash may become less common—not necessarily obsolete, but secondary.

CBDCs won't solve every problem in global finance, nor will they replace traditional banking systems entirely. But they represent a meaningful evolution in how money is issued, transferred, and stored.

This isn't about replacing the old system overnight. It's about adapting it for a digital world—gradually, responsibly, and with a focus on long-term resilience.

The possibilities are still unfolding, and even though it's too early to predict the final shape of this transformation, one thing is clear: CBDCs mark the beginning of a new chapter in monetary innovation.

13

Pause & Policy: Crypto's Maturity Curve

In the shadows of the post-2008 financial crisis—when trust in banks diluted and balance sheets looked like fiction—a name came into existence: Satoshi Nakamoto.

That single name—real or imagined—sparked a revolution. But here's the catch: we still don't know who Satoshi is. A lone genius? A secretive collective? Or, as some conspiracy theorists whisper, a government-backed experiment designed to reset the global financial system?

To this day, crypto equals Bitcoin for most people, and if you don't know who built the foundation, how do you trust the house?

The Pause (Why the Rollercoaster Still Lacks a Seatbelt)

Crypto didn't slow down because the idea was weak. It slowed down because people struggled with things like understanding it, trusting it, and dealing with risk.

1) 💬 The Mislabeling Problem

We called them "cryptocurrencies", then wondered why governments opposed and the public got confused. For generations, currency sat inside the state's monetary perimeter—central banks.

On the flip side, cryptocurrencies—often created by private entities with their own rules—challenge this foundational definition.

Calling them "currency" just doesn't feel right, often causing confusion. Ask someone, "What exactly is a cryptocurrency?" and you're often met with vague or puzzled answers.

Unfortunately, the word 'Crypto Currency' has become so embedded in everyone's mind that re-labeling it now is an uphill task.

2) 📈 Volatility—Emotional Whiplash

Picture waking up feeling low, checking your phone—and seeing your crypto portfolio has doubled overnight. Your heart races. Dreams of early retirement and freedom flood your mind.

Then, the next morning, the same portfolio crashes by 90%. Your stomach sinks. The dream vanishes. You feel betrayed, confused, angry—even questioning your faith in crypto.

It's not just numbers on a screen; it's your future, your savings, your hope. That emotional whiplash is real—and it's a main reason crypto still feels too risky for average folks.

Let's fix the volatility problem, and adoption will automatically grow.

3) 🏛 Unclear Rules—The Unmarked Road

Driving through a city with no traffic rules, no signs, and no limits is no fun. No idea what's legal or dangerous.

That's crypto today for many. Without clear regulations, the space feels lawless. Every day, people wonder if they're walking into opportunity—or a trap.

4) 🧹 Too Much Dirt—Signal vs. Noise

There are millions of cryptocurrencies in existence today. Yes, millions. And no, that's not a good thing. Anyone with a laptop and a latte can launch a token in a matter of hours. That openness is part of what makes crypto exciting; it's also what makes it dangerous.

Think of a market where 99% of products are fake or broken. The ICO money-vacuum era didn't help. People asked: *Is any of this real?* The honest answer: Yes—but only a few projects truly matter. The industry has to keep cleaning houses so the signal can breathe.

5) 🔐 Crypto Is Not Safe: The Fear That Freezes Adoption

What else stops your neighbor or friend from jumping into crypto?

Fear. Fear that Crypto doesn't feel safe.

Countless stories of breaches surface every now and then. Every few months, another exchange hacked. Another wallet drained. Another investor wiped out.

So, people stay away. The fear of losing everything is quite real.

On the contrary, traditional finance never had any such problems. People trade stocks, bonds, and commodities without ever worrying about safety.

Crypto should be no exception.

Security, thus, is a big problem in Crypto that must be solved and solved for good.

Policy Arrives

From Wild West to Rulebook (How Clarity Emerged)

When Bitcoin launched in 2009, it was a rebellion against the financial establishment—a peer-to-peer system designed to bypass banks and governments. For years, crypto lived in a regulatory vacuum.

Regulators barely noticed at first. But as billions poured into crypto markets and disasters like Mt. Gox and FTX shook confidence, lawmakers realized the question wasn't *if* crypto should be regulated—it was *how*.

a) The Early Days

Initially, there were no clear rules. Exchanges operated without licenses, ICOs raised millions with little more than a whitepaper, and fraud was rampant. Regulators tried applying old laws. The result? Confusion and lawsuits.

b) The Shift Toward Clarity

By 2023, global efforts began.

The EU introduced MiCA, the first comprehensive crypto framework.

Similarly, the U.K. is working on the FCA Crypto Framework to define rules and policies.

In the U.S., years of "regulation by enforcement" gave way to legislation. By 2025, three major bills reshaped the landscape:

- **GENIUS Act**: Focused on stablecoin regulations and policy framework.
- **CLARITY Act**: Designed to fix one of the biggest problems in U.S. crypto regulation: Years of uncertainty, overlapping jurisdictions, and regulation-by-enforcement.

The Clarity Act would introduce policies to define digital assets, establish rules around consumer protection, aim to stop illicit finance, fundraising rules, and more.

- **Market Structure Bill**: This bill essentially complements the above two bills. It will propose a full framework for exchanges, custody, and anti-manipulation rules.

The GENIUS Act got passed into law on July 18th, 2025.

The CLARITY and Market Structure Bills have been introduced and are expected to be approved by the Senate in 2026.

And let's not forget the arrival of CBDCs in the earlier chapter. A big step forward that brings greater credibility to digital currencies.

Solving the Classification Puzzle

Crypto assets don't fit neatly into old categories. It's a modern financial instrument that requires a new playbook of rules.

Coming from the U.S., this is a glimpse of what the crypto classification draft looks like. Obviously, it could evolve over time, and different countries could come up with their own versions of it.

- **Commodities**: Bitcoin, Ether, Solana, XRP and more
- **Securities**: ICO tokens with profit expectations
- **Stablecoins**: Regulated under payment and money transmission laws

These classifications matter. They determine who regulates these assets, how they are taxed, and where they can trade.

Banks vs Crypto: The Big Battle

If the crypto industry could offer the same set of products and services that a typical bank does, then it poses a threat to banks. That's 100% true.

If this emerging industry can offer better interest rates, instant and attractive loans, seamless and secure deposits, then Banks and Digital Assets seem to be competing in the same lane.

And therefore, as the rules of this industry are being crafted, regulators all across the globe are going to have a really hard time keeping a balance between "Protecting existing Financial Pillars" vs "Embracing Modern One".

Lobbying from either side will be part of the game as the capital war heats up.

In relation to this very topic, you will also hear this term often – "**Level Playing Field**".

It essentially means the rules should be fair for all. Winners and losers should be picked based on utility and efficiency, and not based on biased policies that favor one over the other.

The Road Ahead

The journey from chaos to clarity seems to be underway.

Regulation isn't the enemy of innovation—it's the foundation for trust. And trust will take crypto from the fringes to the financial mainstream.

It's fair to assume that regulations won't be flawless on day one. They may fall short of what the industry truly needs.

But it's also reasonable to believe that the rules will evolve and mature over time.

Fixing the flaws of a new industry by crafting proper rules is any day better than killing or stalling it.

So, with that spirit of improvement and evolution, let's next talk about something that quietly powers the whole ecosystem.

It may not excite my tech-averse friends as much, but it definitely deserves the spotlight: **Blockchain**.

14

Blockchain – The Engine that Deserves its Space

Before Bitcoin, Before NFTs, Before Wall Street's Embrace…

There was Blockchain.

The silent architect. The invisible backbone. The technology that made everything else possible.

We've spent chapters unpacking coins, tokens, NFTs, and even Wall Street's dramatic entrance into the crypto arena. But none of these stars could shine without the quiet powerhouse working backstage: the blockchain.

To skip over it now would be like reviewing a Ferrari and forgetting to mention the engine that makes it roar.

So yes, this chapter is a tech detour. If you're allergic to tech jargon or simply don't care how the magic works, feel free to skip ahead. This chapter is completely optional for you.

But if curiosity is your thing, buckle up—because understanding blockchain is like peeking behind the curtain of this new financial instrument.

What Exactly Is Blockchain?

Imagine a public notebook in a town square:

- There's a giant notebook in the center of town.
- Anyone can write down a transaction: *"Alice gave Bob ₹500."*
- Once written, the entry cannot be erased or changed—it's permanent.
- Every new page contains a unique code linked to the previous; tampering with one page would break the chain.
- Everyone can see the notebook, making it transparent.
- But instead of names, people use unique codes (wallet addresses), so it's private yet public.

This notebook works like a blockchain:

- Pages are blocks
- Notebook is the chain
- The unique code is a hash
- Town is the global network of computers

Blockchain Cheat Sheet

If you want a quick primer, here are some key terms:

- **Mining**: validating transactions and adding them to the blockchain.
- **Nodes**: computers that maintain and verify the blockchain.
- **Hashing**: encrypting data into a fixed-length code.
- **Proof-of-Work**: a method requiring computational effort to validate transactions.

In essence, Blockchain is a distributed ledger—a digital record book shared across thousands of computers worldwide. Every transaction is recorded in blocks, chained together in chronological order, and secured with cryptography.

No single entity owns it, and no one can secretly alter it.

Blockchain exists in multiple forms beyond its origins with Bitcoin as a public network. Today, private and hybrid blockchains have emerged, designed to meet specific needs such as enhanced privacy, governance, and organizational control.

Let's also check out the "Summary Table" below that reflects different layers of blockchain

☑ Summary Table

Layer	Purpose	Examples
L0	Base infrastructure, interoperability, networking	Polkadot, Cosmos, Celestia
L1	Main blockchains, consensus, settlement	Bitcoin, Ethereum, Solana
L2	Scaling & speed improvements	Polygon, Arbitrum, Optimism
L3	Applications & smart contracts	Uniswap, OpenSea, Aave

How to Judge a Blockchain

The Big Five:

1. **Speed** – Fast transaction processing.
2. **Cost** – Affordable fees.
3. **Decentralization** – Resistance to censorship.
4. **Scalability** – Ability to handle growth.
5. **Security** – Robust and safe from exploits or hacks.

The holy grail? A blockchain that nails all five.

Different blockchains rely on different consensus models to keep everyone on the same page.

Conclusion: Blockchain, the silent Hero

Blockchain isn't flashy like NFTs or dramatic like memecoins. It doesn't trend on Twitter every day. But it's the backbone—the quiet force rewriting the rules of trust, ownership, and value.

Ignore it, and you miss the essence of crypto. Understand it, and you see the future unfolding.

Because blockchain isn't just powering crypto—it's expanding use cases for supply chains, healthcare, identity systems, and even voting.

Here are a few examples of how blockchain is already helping solve different industry problems beyond Finance.

1. Supply Chain & Logistics

Impact: End-to-end transparency, tamper-proof tracking, and reduced fraud.

Example:

- **IBM Food Trust** uses blockchain to **trace the journey of food** from farm to store, improving safety and recall efficiency.

2. Healthcare

Impact: Secure patient data sharing & tamper-proof medical records.

Example:

- **MediLedger** enables **verified drug traceability**, preventing counterfeit medicines.

3. Real Estate

Impact: Tokenization, fractional ownership, faster property transfers.

Example:

Propy allows **blockchain-based property sales**, reducing document fraud and weeks of manual paperwork.

4. Government & Public Sector

Impact: Transparent, tamper-proof records & improved citizen trust.

Example:

- **Estonia's e-Governance system** stores **citizen records on blockchain**, making ID and public services ultra-secure.

5. Voting & Elections

Impact: Fraud-proof digital voting systems.

Example:

- **Voatz** used blockchain-based voting in **U.S. pilot elections**, enabling secure remote voting.

While we uncovered a few examples, use cases expand to other sectors like Energy, Education, Transportation, and more.

An important point worth calling out here – Blockchain isn't the only decentralized ledger solution out there. Some non-blockchain DLTs claim faster transaction speeds and lower energy use.

DLT stands for Distributed Ledger Technology. It's a system that distributes a ledger across multiple participants, ensuring synchronization and security without a central authority. Examples include blockchain, Hashgraph, and Directed Acyclic Graph (DAG) systems.

In summary: Blockchain is a *specific type* of DLT, but DLT encompasses a wider range of decentralized ledger technologies beyond blockchain.

Governments and banks often explore wholesale CBDCs using DLT frameworks that may not rely on blockchain.

With DLT and blockchain, we've laid the foundation of trust and transparency in the digital age.

As we close this chapter, remember—what you've explored here is only the beginning. If this technology sparks your curiosity, don't stop now.

The web is rich with deeper insights, advanced concepts, and real-world applications waiting to be discovered.

This chapter merely scratched the surface; the journey ahead holds far more to uncover.

Now, let's turn the page to explore the promise of modern finance, where innovation reshapes the way value moves across the world.

15
The Promise of Modern Finance

If there's one thing we can all agree on, it's this: NFTs and Memes were never meant to be the cornerstone of crypto.

They were fun, sure—but not the real deal. The true promise of this technology lies far beyond digital art and internet jokes."

Every time I would read stories of how a meme or a shiny new token soared, it left me baffled rather than thrilled.

So, let's dive into the real-world challenges that digital assets can help solve.

For decades, we've relied on systems built in the 20th century—slow, expensive, and closed off.

But now, the future is knocking.

It's time to modernize the outdated financial system using DLTs and crypto instruments.

🌐 The Vision

Imagine a world where money moves as fast and freely as information does today.

But the reality? The traditional financial system is stuck in the past.

It's slow. It's expensive. It's full of friction.

This friction makes it nearly impossible for a business to send $100 million to a partner across the globe in seconds or even minutes.

In fact, the fastest way today might be to board a plane and carry the money physically.

Insane, right?

💸 Trillions Locked in the Old System

Think about this: trillions of dollars are sitting idle in the old, traditional banking system, especially in something called Nostro/Vostro accounts.

What are these Nostro/Vostro accounts?

They're special accounts that banks use to handle money in foreign currencies. For example, if an Indian bank wants to send money in dollars, it keeps an account with a U.S. bank—and vice versa.

Here's the problem though:

To make sure international payments don't fail, banks must park huge amounts of money in these accounts, just waiting to be used.

Not a few million.

Not even a few billion.

Trillions.

And that money just sits there—doing nothing—instead of being used for loans, businesses, or economic growth.

This is where DLT comes in.

It's designed to let money move instantly and securely across borders—without needing banks to lock away massive piles of cash. That means less waste and more money flowing through the economy.

🕒 Why Are Markets Still Sleeping?

We've come to terms with an outdated ritual: markets opening and closing like theater curtains, granting stocks, bonds, treasuries, etc., a mere 7–8 hours on stage.

That's been the rule for decades. But why?

Why can't we trade stocks 24/7, like crypto? Why not on weekends?

Why do settlements still take days?

It's like waiting for a letter in the age of email.

👷 Real-Time Finance for Real Life

We've grown used to paychecks arriving once or twice a month. But what if that cadence changed?

What if they could get paid every week or every day?

With real-time settlements costing just pennies, that's all very much possible.

🚀 The Promise of Blockchain Finance

Blockchain isn't just technology; it's a new financial operating system.

It promises:

- Speed
- Transparency
- Global access

- Unprecedented efficiency

This future isn't distant.

🛠 Rebuilding the Foundations

As you explore this world more, you'll often hear phrases like:

- "Upgrading or plumbing of old financial system."
- "Building new financial guardrails."
- "Replacing legacy financial infrastructure."

These aren't just buzzwords.

They reflect a deep shift from paper-driven processes to programmable money and smart contracts.

🔗 Tokenization: The Game-Changer

Tokenization is the process of converting real-world value into digital tokens.

Tokens can represent:

- 🏠 Real estate
- 🎨 Art
- 🏦 Bonds
- 🥇 Commodities
- 🌱 Carbon credits
- 💎 Luxury goods

Tokenization also enables fractional ownership, global access, and seamless trading—all on blockchain.

Want a piece of a Dubai skyscraper? Or a share in a rare painting?

Maybe just a few milligrams of gold because the full bar costs a fortune? Even fractional stocks and bonds?

Tokenization is about to flip the script on ownership—changing how we buy, sell, and trade assets forever.

Reputed research predicts tokenization will reach tens of trillions of dollars within five years, and calls that just the beginning.

💸 Earn, Lend, Borrow

In this new financial ecosystem:

- Your money doesn't just sit—it works for you.
- Earn interest on crypto deposits through decentralized finance (DeFi) platforms.
- Lend crypto and earn passive income.
- Borrow money using crypto as collateral—without selling your assets.

It's like turning your wallet into a bank, an investment fund, and a credit line—all at once.

🌍 A Borderless Future

This isn't just innovation—it's reinvention.

Finance is becoming:

- Open
- Programmable
- Global
- Efficient

Institutions are ready. Infrastructure is evolving.

Check out some stats that show how far and wide crypto has reached.

Key Statistics

- According to Crypto.com, more than 9% of the global population (~700+ million) owns crypto.
- Many countries, including the U.S., U.K., and European nations legally embrace crypto.
- 100s of public firms and dozens of private firms now hold crypto on their balance sheets.
- Several financial institutions like J.P. Morgan have already launched stablecoins, while many others are actively preparing to introduce their own.
- Crypto giants like Coinbase, Circle, and Gemini have launched IPOs, with many more anticipated in the coming years.
- Major retail, tech, travel, and entertainment companies accept crypto payments via third-party processors—including the likes of Amazon, Microsoft, Tesla, PayPal, Home Depot.
- Mastercard and Visa are now actively working on embedding crypto into global payment networks through stablecoin rails, crypto-linked cards, and broad partnerships.
- Countries like El Salvador, the UAE, and Germany offer tax-friendly crypto environments, fueling adoption.
- Several governments themselves have begun investing in crypto. With national debts climbing year after year, several countries are now exploring and investing in digital assets as a potential strategic tool to ease their fiscal burdens.
- E-commerce giants like Shopify and Stripe support stablecoin payments.

To summarize; above statistics is more than just data. It's a reflection of how far this industry has come in terms of adoption.

Are we fully there yet? No. Absolutely not.

Are we headed there? Well, that's the story data tells us.

I would like to pause here for a moment, as this might be the right time to bring up a question.

A question that my mind keeps returning to:

Can we build the new financial highway without crypto?

The idea of modern finance without crypto at the center of it?

Possibly.

But so far, no other solution has yet emerged to tackle the deep flaws in our current financial system.

Maybe tomorrow brings a new contender. Maybe another path to modern finance appears.

But right now, it looks like "DLT + Crypto" are the brave kids out there, raising their hands and saying – "Hey, we can make it happen!"

16

A Guide You May Need

I often wish I had a playbook back in 2016 when I first stumbled upon Bitcoin. But those were uncharted days—even the industry itself had no idea what shape it would eventually take or where it would stand a decade later as we step into 2026.

Satoshi himself couldn't have imagined that one day his experiment would become the foundation for a trillion-dollar industry, reshaping how the world thinks about money, value, and trust.

Fast-forward to today, and phrases that once sounded radical are becoming part of mainstream conversations:

- Bitcoin is digital gold
- DeFi redefining traditional banking
- Nations holding strategic reserves of digital assets
- Stablecoins powering instant global payments
- CBDCs
- New Financial Infrastructure

Countries like the U.S. have opened the door for crypto investments in retirement accounts like IRAs and 401(k)s. And that is huge.

Every now and then, there's a story of a new nation joining and embracing digital assets. Not just big names, but smaller countries like Bhutan and Taiwan too.

And 2026 is shaping up to be a promising year for digital-asset regulation.

Once this space is properly regulated, trust will follow—from the masses, institutions, and global markets. With trust comes adoption, and with adoption comes growth.

So, in that spirit, let me share a practical guide to help you make smarter, safer decisions if you choose to invest in digital assets.

1. Educate Yourself Relentlessly

This industry isn't static—it's an ocean in motion. New protocols, use cases, and technologies emerge almost daily. Staying informed isn't optional—it's essential.

Focus on core use cases with long-term utility and regulatory viability.

Here's the list of some key financial use cases that matter

- Faster, cheaper cross-border payments with real time settlement
- Tokenization of assets—from stocks to real estate to art
- Automated lending, borrowing, yield
- Custody and treasury solutions
- Privacy-focused solutions

Skip the hype. Meme Coins may trend, but utility wins in the long run.

2. Evaluate Projects Like a Venture Capitalist

Crypto isn't a casino. It's not winner-takes-all. Just as the internet birthed giants like Amazon and Google, crypto will have many winners across diverse verticals.

Ask the hard questions:

- Is the project solving a genuine Business problem?
- Green light from regulators?
- Where does it fit in the new Financial Infrastructure?
- Can it bridge the gap between Traditional and Modern Finance?
- Are there any live products and partnerships driving real-world utility?
- Can it scale, and is it safe from hacks?

Apply the same diligence you'd use for any startup. Except the pace is faster, and the stakes are higher.

3. Diversify Your Investment Approach

Crypto investments are becoming more accessible and legitimate. You no longer need obscure exchanges or complex self-custody to participate.

Consider three primary categories:

- **Direct Crypto Investments:** Buy and hold digital assets on proven regulated exchanges or secure hardware wallets.
- **Crypto ETFs and Index Funds:** This is another good option. Expect a surge in crypto ETFs and Index fund offerings in the coming years, offering diversified exposure with lower risk.
- **Equity in Crypto Companies:** Crypto companies like Coinbase and Circle went public with a lot of buzz and

excitement, and are doing fairly well. Many more are expected to follow in the coming years.

Investing in IPO stocks of promising crypto companies can be a smart way to avoid direct exposure to cryptocurrencies while still benefiting from the industry's growth potential.

4. Understand Tokenomics Before You Invest

Tokenomics forms the foundation of every crypto project. It explains how a currency operates and whether its model is sustainable.

Key indicators—such as Market Cap, Circulating Supply, and Total Supply—are essential for evaluating long-term viability. Make it a habit to study tokenomics whenever you evaluate a crypto project.

5. Stay Vigilant and Adaptive

In crypto, change is the only constant.

The hottest project today might be a forgotten coin tomorrow.

Exchanges rise and fall, governments rewrite the rules, and founders sometimes disappear overnight.

To survive, you must stay vigilant, keep learning, and always be prepared to move.

6. Macro Signals That Move Crypto: Sentiment, News, and Big Wallets

Crypto markets are highly sensitive to macroeconomic and geopolitical forces. Negative headlines—or even speculation—can hit this asset class harder than most.

Wars, tariffs, and government shutdowns often ripple through prices. A single tweet from a major figure can spark volatility. Interest rate decisions and liquidity conditions are closely watched, shaping investor sentiment.

The 'Fear and Greed Index' captures this psychological pulse, ranging from 1 to 100: high scores signal optimism and greed, while low scores reflect fear—and markets often move accordingly.

Then there are the whales—the market movers. It's unfortunate but true that a significant share of digital assets belongs to a handful of people called whales. When these whales sell or even shift coins, panic can spread across the market within minutes.

In crypto, understanding psychology and power dynamics is just as important as reading charts.

7. Avoid Leverage Trading

If you thrive on risk and enjoy trying to predict the future, remember this: keep emotions in check and steer clear of leverage. The crypto market is notoriously volatile and often defies expectations.

Just when you're certain of the trend, prices can swing violently in the opposite direction. Even seasoned traders have lost millions through leveraged bets.

Unless you have surplus capital you can truly afford to lose, avoiding leverage is a wise move in crypto.

8. Protect Your Digital Assets

As we discussed in earlier chapters, the safety of digital assets remains one of the biggest challenges in the crypto world. Always choose trusted, reputable platforms—and never put all eggs in one basket.

Maybe keep a portion on a reliable centralized exchange, another portion on decentralized platforms, and some on a hardware wallet.

Also, don't skip the basics that often get overlooked but make all the difference in the long run:

- Store your private keys securely. Lose the keys, and you lose the coins—there's no recovery hotline in crypto.

- Use strong passwords and enable robust security features like Google Authenticator or other multi-factor authentication tools.
- Protect your devices with reliable antivirus software, keeping malware and phishing threats at bay.

Last but not least, putting your crypto up as collateral to borrow more may feel tempting, but it's a dangerous move. Markets can turn in an instant—and with one sharp drop, your collateral could vanish.

9. Last but Not Least: Patience Is Your Greatest Ally

Crypto is a marathon, not a hundred-meter dash. Prices can flatline for years with no major action. Some seasons are filled with daily excitement and constant movement; others feel like the market has fallen into deep sleep.

Patience is part of the journey.

As we wrap up this guide, remember one thing: crypto may be built on code, but surviving it is an art. The landscape you're stepping into is far more evolved than what existed in 2016, yet the essence remains unchanged—curiosity rewards you; complacency punishes you, and patience defines you.

This chapter isn't a flawless road map, because crypto doesn't offer any. But it is the playbook I wish someone had handed me years ago—a compass to help you navigate chaos with confidence.

Take it. Use it. Add to it. And let it guide you toward becoming not just an investor, but a thoughtful steward.

The Curtains Fall

And just like that, the curtain gently falls on this journey we've taken together. Strange, isn't it?

That unforgettable Bitcoin dinner date still felt fresh in my memory, as if it had happened yesterday. Yet here we were, about to wrap up the crypto journey.

How something that began with curiosity and confusion now ends with clarity, conviction, and a quiet sense of purpose.

I won't lie—there's a bittersweet feeling in writing these final words.

This book has been more than pages and paragraphs. It's been a reflection of my own journey—my mistakes, my wins, and my lessons.

So yes, there's a tinge of sadness as we reach the last chapter. But more than that, there's a deep gratitude—for the journey, for the growth, and for the chance to share a story that I hope now becomes a part of yours.

I hope this book has sparked something in you—a desire to learn, to question, to explore. Because the world of crypto isn't just about charts and coins, it's about rewriting the rules of finance.

A new industry is rising—bringing jobs and shaping possibilities that don't fully exist yet.

Hence, let's remember and acknowledge that this emerging industry is not just about investment and price charts. The opportunities expand far beyond.

You could be a Blockchain developer crafting smart contracts. You can build digital wallets that can hold Digital Assets, CBDC's, ETFs and tokenized assets at one single place.

You can be a consultant guiding businesses into Web3, an NFT artist, a crypto journalist, or a tutor helping others decode this complex world.

So go ahead. Step out. Explore this new world the way it suits you best.

And I hope your best chapters are still ahead.

P.S. Before you close this book, flip through the final pages. I've handpicked a list of fun facts just for you—from legendary crypto blunders to billion-dollar pizzas. These stories are quirky, surprising, and fun!

And with that… I'll leave you to it.

Fun Facts

📜 Fun Fact 1 – 2009: The Genesis Block

In 2009, the very first Bitcoin block was mined—the Genesis Block.

Embedded inside was a subtle, powerful message:

"The Times 03/Jan/2009 Chancellor on brink of second bailout for banks."

A quiet protest against centralized finance, it marked the birth of Bitcoin and ignited a revolution.

Fun Fact 2 – May 22: Bitcoin Pizza Day

On May 22, 2010, programmer Laszlo Hanyecz made history with the first documented real-world Bitcoin purchase.

He paid 10,000 Bitcoins for two Papa John's pizzas—worth about $41 back then.

Every May 22, the crypto community celebrates with pizza parties, giveaways, and reflections on this incredible journey—from cheesy slices to serious systems.

And that leads us to the second image in this book:

Someone buying a Domino's Pizza Gift Card worth $18 by paying 19.12 Bitcoins. This was the time when 1 Bitcoin was priced at around 95 cents.

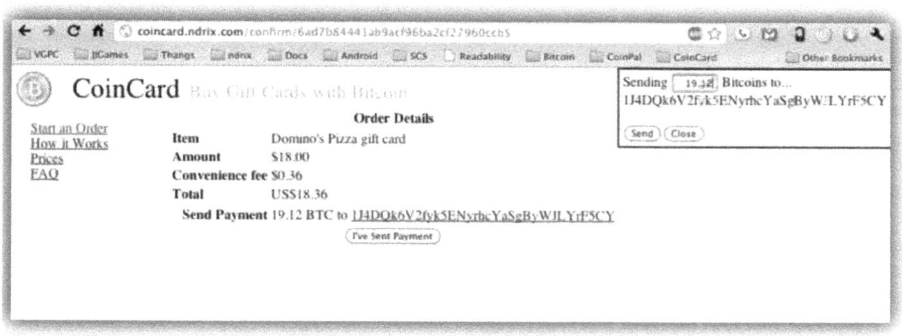

Fun Fact 3 – The Billion-Dollar Meme Coin Donation

In May 2021, Vitalik Buterin, Ethereum's co-founder, donated 50 trillion SHIB tokens to India's COVID-19 relief fund. The value of that donation was worth over $1 billion at that time.

Yes, a meme coin helped fight a real-world pandemic. Let that sink in.

📅 Fun Fact 4 – 2013: James Howells and The Buried Bitcoin

In one of crypto's most expensive mistakes, James Howells, an IT worker from Wales, accidentally threw away a hard drive in 2013.

On that drive? The private keys to 8,000 Bitcoins.

Once a minor loss, it's now a digital treasure worth hundreds of millions—buried somewhere in a Newport landfill.

After 12 years of failed attempts to recover the hard drive, Howells eventually gave up on his pursuit as the city council refused a full excavation.

James's story is a modern crypto legend—a haunting reminder that your keys are your coins, and one careless moment can cost a fortune.

🔓 Fun Fact 5 – The Lost Passwords of Crypto Millionaires

It's estimated that roughly 15 to 20% of all Bitcoin is lost forever—locked away in wallets whose owners forgot their passwords or lost private keys.

One famous case is Stefan Thomas, a German-born programmer who received 7,002 BTC in 2011 as payment for making an explainer video about Bitcoin. Unfortunately, he stored the private keys on an IronKey hardware wallet and later forgot the password.

The device allows only a limited number of attempts before permanently locking, and Thomas has just **two guesses left**. Because of this, he has kept the drive in a secure vault, hoping that future advances in technology might one day allow him to recover the funds.

💎 Fun Fact 6 – Famous Metaverse Sale: The ~$4.3 million Sandbox Estate

In November 2021, **Republic Realm** made headlines by purchasing a massive 24×24 estate in **The Sandbox** for a jaw-dropping **~$4.3 million**.

This wasn't just a plot of virtual land—it became part of their ambitious project called **Fantasy Islands**, featuring luxury villas and even virtual jet skis! This sale remains one of the most iconic examples of how digital real estate can rival physical property prices.

💡 Fun Fact 7 – North Korea, The Hacking Powerhouse

After years of cyber heists and exchange hacks, North Korea is now believed to own a large quantity of Bitcoins placing it among the largest national Bitcoin reserves worldwide.

In February 2025, its Lazarus Group carried out the biggest crypto theft to date, draining $1.5 billion from the Bybit exchange.

The scale of that attack sent shockwaves through the industry, and today, nearly every major crypto platform treats Lazarus with extreme caution.

⌛ Fun Fact 8 – The 2024 Bitcoin Halving Surprise

For the first time, 2024 broke the 4-year Bitcoin Halving trend as the much-anticipated price surge didn't happen.

The expected rally didn't come, leaving analysts scratching their heads. In crypto, nothing is guaranteed—except change.

🎉 Fun Fact 9 – You're Officially Awesome 😎

Finishing a book isn't easy. Most people start and never finish. That's more commitment than most gym memberships.

By finishing this book, you've minted a priceless NFT: a smarter you.

Go ahead—give yourself a high-five (or a crypto fist bump).

Thank You, Reader.

"Until Next Time!!!"

Scan QR Code or
Send email to provide feedback

Email: bookbyvipul@gmail.com

www.ingramcontent.com/pod-product-compliance
Lightning Source LLC
LaVergne TN
LVHW050937210926
848482LV00013B/648
* 9 7 9 8 9 0 3 1 9 7 4 8 4 *